The Poorhouses and Poor Farms of Michigan

Alan Naldrett

With Introduction by David Blaine

In the Charles Dickens' book Oliver Twist, Oliver is in the
poorhouse and is ridiculed for asking for more food.

New Naldrett Press

Poor House Kitchen

DEDICATION

This book is dedicated to David Blaine, Cynthia Donahue, and Don Green, who all gave me a lot of instruction and information on the Poor Houses and Farms of Michigan!

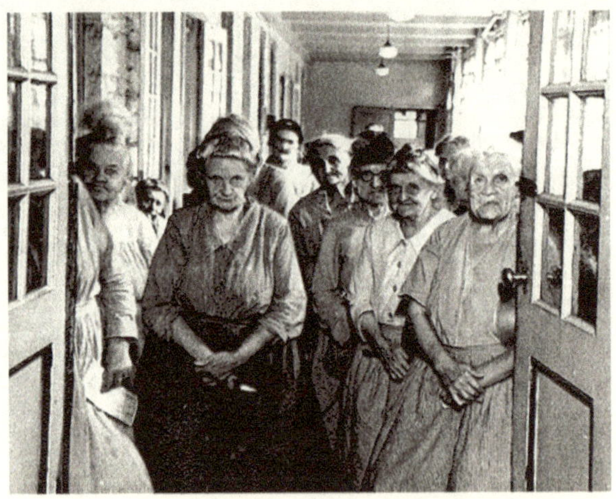

Copyright 2019 by Alan Naldrett

ISBN 9781707599394

CONTENTS

INTRODUCTION

The British Poor Laws

English Common Law came in large part from the Bible. In the Gospel of Matthew, Chapter 25, there is a stanza where Jesus says, "For I was hungry, and you fed me. I was thirsty, and you gave me a drink. I was a stranger, and you invited me into your home. I was naked, and you gave me clothing. I was sick, and you cared for me. I was in prison, and you visited me.'" In England this was distilled to a list of the "corporal works of mercy. "They are:

(1) Feed the hungry.
(2) Give drink to the thirsty.
(3) Clothe the naked.
(4) Shelter the homeless.
(5) Visit those in prison.
(6) Comfort the sick.
(7) Bury the dead.

There is also mention of an 8th about welcoming the stranger, but this one fell by the wayside. When Henry the VIII expelled the Catholic Church and confiscated their lands, a lot of unemployed priests and nuns abounded. At the same time, new agricultural methods were throwing field hands out of work.

King Henry wasn't as concerned with the well-being of the unemployed as much as he was that they might gather together and start a revolt. In 1563, Justices of the Peace were authorized to raise funds through taxes for the relief of the poor.

The poor were placed into different categories. The first was the "Helpless Poor," which included widows, children, and the elderly, sick, and disabled. The next category was the "Able-Bodied Poor." These were people who could work, and wanted to work, but were jobless due to high unemployment. And the third, and last, category was "Rogues and Vagabonds."

This third group was often made up of criminals and beggars. Begging was often a disguise for thievery, and begging was outlawed. (Although some who were deemed genuinely worthy were granted begging licenses by the Parrish.) Some punishments for being caught as a vagabond were whipping, hanging, branding of the tongue, being placed in stocks, and even being sold into slavery. The government felt that this group of people were most likely to instigate a peasant revolt and these severe punishments were formed as prevention as well as punishment.

The townspeople also held beggars in low esteem and treated them badly, because it was the townspeople who fell prey to the criminal element. In 1556 a beggar named Nicholas Jennings was caught in London with a bag of blood. He was using it to paint fake wounds on his head. He was found to be collecting a daily sum that would take an ordinary workman two weeks to earn.

In 1572 a local property tax called the "Poor Rate" was imposed to raise funds for the relief of the poor.

In 1576 the idea of a workhouse was first suggested, to act as a deterrent to asking for relief.

In 1597 Overseers of the Poor were appointed.

In 1601 the Elizabethan Poor Law was created. This restated many things already in play, notably compulsory poor taxes, to be collected from the owners of real property. Also, the creation of the overseers of the poor, and the concept of "setting the poor on work."

Overseers were to decide how much money was needed for local relief, to collect the taxes, relieve the poor and supervise the parish poor house. Eventually every Parish had a poor house, although they went by various names—poorhouse (sometimes spelled with two words-poor house), Almshouse, Asylum, County Farm, County Infirmary, and Poor Farm, to name a few.

Relief was divided between indoor relief and outdoor relief. Whether you qualified for relief was decided by the overseers, and what type of relief you were offered depended on the category of poor you were placed in. It should be noted that overseers were appointed each year at Easter, were unpaid, and had rarely been poor themselves. Some were less empathetic than others. Research shows that overseers were often land owners, which means the people paying the taxes also determined who would get help and how much.

- The deserving poor were often given outdoor relief, allowing them to stay out of the poor house and remain in their homes. This type of aid often consisted of food and clothing.
- The infirm that could not take care of themselves were placed in the poor house.
- The unemployed who wanted work could be put to work in a workhouse.
- The undeserving poor were auctioned off into indentured servitude or, later, placed in work houses or farms, and later houses of correction. (This was not always voluntary.)

There was a major but not obvious change in the Elizabethan Poor Law. The previous poor laws were a collection of acts, but this new Act was an integrated law, and where in the past people who would not work but could were often punished, the newer view was that they were to be corrected. Poverty was beginning to be viewed as a moral failing, and wealth was beginning to be viewed as a divine blessing. This view came about as Protestantism spread in Europe.

Since control was local, there were variations and stricter or laxer interpretations and enforcement of poor laws, but there was always a concept that family members were responsible for one another. Parents were to live with children and sometimes outdoor relief made that possible.

In 1662 the Settlement Act brought the local nature of assistance to the fore. The Settlement Act required the poor person to establish residence by living in the Parish for a specified time before receiving relief. Poor not deemed local could be removed, sent back to their last Parish of residence, or Parish of birth. This was especially difficult for women, who were not considered citizens. Women had to apply in the parish of their husband, or if single, their father, or in the absence of either, go back to their parish of birth.

At this point the systems of social welfare and criminal justice seem to share a ride. Part of the Settlement Act had the effect of keeping criminals out of the Parish. Many of those deemed able to work but wouldn't were categorized as "sturdy beggars." People were advised not to give alms to beggars, and eventually some areas even passed laws making it a crime.

If these able-bodied poor were not settled or were not locals, they would be "removed" or sent to a workhouse. If they could not be sent anywhere else, they could be sent to a house of correction where they could be forced into work. And those were the lucky ones! They were sometimes stoned and beaten until they ran past the stones marking the parish border. If they came back, they were hanged.

Some aspects of the Poor House that carried over into the criminal justice system were that the occupants were called "inmates," and that they were often clothed in uniforms, especially in workhouses, and later houses of correction. They were not always voluntarily admitted, nor could they always leave when they wished.

The overall system served the English people well in their time and place, but there were a few criticisms. For one, the poor rate was only levied against land and buildings, so there were many who paid no tax. Of more important concern was that the worthy poor were placed in poor houses with bad influences. You had children living with the mentally ill and criminals. Eventually some people would be brought out of poor houses and placed in more appropriate institutions such as orphanages and mental asylums.

As in any "institution" there were instances of impropriety. In some instances, inmates were overworked, underfed, beaten, raped, given inadequate medical attention and generally mistreated in any way you might imagine.

In brief recap, English Poor Laws were built on the principles that:

- They did not help the able-bodied poor.
- Family members were required to help their poor relatives.
- The local parish helped their local poor.
- The able-bodied poor were put to work.

The Elizabethan Poor Laws made their way across the Atlantic to the state of Vermont. Prior to adopting the laws, Vermont residents made it very hard on the indignant—jailing them, selling them into indentured servitude, and sometimes hanging them! So, when Vermont adopted the Elizabethan Poor Laws it was a step up from what they had done prior to that.

Along with the English laws Vermont had also adopted the English attitudes that poverty was a personal failing and needed correcting. The first poor laws in Vermont authorized towns to establish work houses and houses of correction. These places were for, "… keeping, correcting and setting to work vagrants, common beggars, and lewd, idle and disorderly persons."

As strict as this was, the citizens of Vermont were eager to do right by their less fortunate citizens. By 1799 they had voted to set aside one percent of taxes for the selectmen to care for the needs of the poor, including a Christian burial. Prior to that, the selectmen had taken care of their poverty problem by auctioning the poor off to the best bidder. That was eventually seen as failing the old, sick, children and the mentally ill.

In 1831 Vermonters voted to fund a poor house and one was built, only to be abandoned in 1875 due to disrepair. A new poor farm was then built on 400 acres, out of sight of the general population, which was the custom.

In 1884 forty-seven inmates were housed there at an annual cost of about $3,600. Poor farms — which were often exactly that, where strong-bodied male "inmates" were put to work as farmhands and the women as kitchen-hands — were considered a last, and far from desirable, resort. Vermonters, it was said, were raised with a reverence for God, the hope of heaven, and a fear of the poorhouse.

The poorhouse ideology of Vermont spread over the various states, including Michigan, and soon most had passed legislation regarding the building of poorhouses and poor farms.

---David Blaine

David Blaine is an historian and President of the Sanilac County Historical Society.

London Poor House in the Elizabethan style of architecture

FOREWORD

Michigan began enacting laws regarding indigent people when, under Michigan's Northwest Territory Act of 1790, counties were divided into townships and each township assigned an "Overseer of the Poor." The Overseer's duties were defined as inquiring about the poor families in his jurisdiction. He was then expected to report to the Justice of the Peace anyone who was likely to become a public charge, and then to provide "proper and reasonable relief" to the poor person.

When Michigan became an official territory in 1805, a 10-page document titled *Act for the Relief of the Poor* was passed. This law allowed the Overseer to auction off care of the indigent to the lowest bidder. This was a system that originally came from England and had been around for over a hundred years. It was called the *vendue system* and was a form of indentured slavery. The auction winner was obligated to feed, house and clothe the indigent, but in return could have them work at whatever job the winning bidder wanted them to.

In 1818, aid for the apprenticeship for young children was provided. In 1827, laws regarding "Bastardy" and the return of runaway slaves were addressed.

In 1830 Michigan enacted its "Poor House Laws," laws that were enacted to require the Board of Supervisors for each county to build accommodations to provide for the well-being of their poor residents. These were defined as laws to help "those who were in need, lacking living quarters, or unable to support themselves." When Michigan achieved statehood in 1837, these laws were strengthened.

However, an 1896 source mentions that Alger, Arenac, Baraga, Benzie, Kalkaska, Leelanau, Montmorency, Oscoda, Presque Isle, and Roscommon Counties did not yet have a facility to house the poor, although many of these counties eventually did have poorhouses or farms. The reason most of these counties didn't have poorhouses was the lack of paupers. Most of the populations of these counties were so low that most indigents that came there were probably taken care of by their families. If they didn't have any family in the area, they were usually driven off to another county.

Most sources list 82 Michigan poorhouses, but in 1885 Alger County broke off from Schoolcraft County and became the 83rd county in Michigan and the last to have a Poorhouse/Farm.

As stated in the introduction, for the most part, facilities would spell "Poorhouse" as one word, although some officially made it two words, "Poor House." Other names for the poorhouse would be the almshouse, County Home, County Poor Farm, County Asylum, and similar.

Many times the inhabitants of the poor farm would be referred to as "inmates," such as in a prison, which in many cases it was. Other names used were paupers, residents, or just "the poor." The non-medical people who worked in a poorhouse facility were usually called "attendants."

It was considered tragic to be assigned to the poorhouse. Many paupers asked to be escorted there in the dead of night so as not to be seen. Once assigned to the poorhouse, many counties would sell all of the indigents' possessions to pay their debts.

Many poorhouses worked on the principle that able-bodied indigents were expected to work for their food and lodging and faced imprisonment if they didn't. Most worked on typical farms but some were sent to "workhouses" or "work farms" and lived there. These were facilities with only the bare essentials. The idea was to make poverty extremely unappealing, as if it wasn't already for most people.

"Workhouses" weren't prevalent in Michigan, although there were some, mostly work farms. Michigan did pass laws to officially provide for workhouses. One was the *Public Act 78 of 1917* which was defined as, "An act to establish and to provide for the conduct and maintenance of *work farms*, factories or shops in counties of this state and to authorize the confinement of convicted persons therein and to provide for the punishment of such persons for breaking or attempting to break out; and to permit counties not operating *work farms*, factories or shops to contract for the care of their prisoners with counties operating such farms, factories or shops." This act was adopted in 1917.

Also part of *Public Act 78* was that "It shall be the duty of the sheriff, constable or other officer in and for any county having such agreement with said commissioners, to whom any warrant or commitment for that purpose may be directed by any court or magistrate in such county, to convey such person so sentenced to the said *work farm*, factory or shop and there deliver such person to the superintendent or other proper officer of the said work farm, factory or shop, whose duty it shall be to receive such person so sentenced and to safely keep and employ such person for the term mentioned in the warrant or commitment, according to the rules and regulations of the said *work farm*, factory or shop; the officer thus conveying and so delivering the person or persons so sentenced shall be allowed such fees or compensation therefore as shall be prescribed or allowed by the board of supervisors for the county in which such persons shall have been convicted." (I have added the italics to the term "work farm.")

Victorian-type workhouse

Residents were often fed unpalatable food and received only a bare bones diet. They were given uncomfortable bedding and the buildings they slept in were often unclean and crowded. In the daytime, the men were put to work breaking stones, cutting wood or similar work.

One of the most common workhouse tasks given to men was crushing bones, so that they could be used for fertilizer. There were cases where the men were so hungry, fights would break out when men wanted to eat the rotting meat still on the bones and suck the marrow remaining in them and didn't want to share the feast.

Females were mostly given domestic labor jobs, including spinning cloth, cleaning, cooking, making beds, and doing laundry.

Poorhouses and Poor Farms began to decline after the Social Security Act of 1935 passed, and by the 1950s most poor facilities had closed. Section 8 housing, homeless shelters and other welfare programs helped fill the gaps.

However, in Michigan, the Ottawa County Poor Farm and a few infirmaries were still being used in the 1980s. In Texas, where poorhouses were called the "Manual Labor Poor House," they lasted until the 1970s. In New Hampshire, there were poorhouses into the 1990s. In Beaufort County, North Carolina, a poorhouse lasted until 2001.

Tewksbury Almshouse was a famous (infamous) state poorhouse in Massachusetts. (The only other state to have a "state poorhouse" was Rhode Island.) Anne Sullivan, teacher of Helen Keller, spent ten years in Tewksbury in the 1860s. It was described by her as "a crime against childhood." She also said, "I doubt if life, or eternity for that matter, is long enough to erase the errors and ugly blots scored upon my brain by those dismal years," speaking about her poorhouse years.

She described the buildings as "ramshackle." Anne slept on an iron cot in a large dormitory building with other orphans. Giant rats would run through the spaces between beds. There was little for them to do, so the residents mostly "milled around like forgotten animals."

Other famous people who spent time in poorhouses were Charlie Chaplin (while still a boy living in England), Calamity Jane, and Annie Oakley. Many stories abounded of formerly wealthy people losing their money and ending up in the Poorhouse.

New York City's first institution for dependent people, the "House of Correction, Workhouse and Poorhouse," opened in 1736. Relatives of the residents were required to help provide much of the resident's expenses. This institution was renamed Bellevue, and eventually became Bellevue Hospital. The Cook County Almshouse in Chicago became the Cook County Hospital. Many of Michigan's poor facilities transitioned into medical centers.

Some of the most notorious poorhouse stories are from the 17th and 18th Century accounts from Great Britain, the years Charles Dickens wrote about. One actual poorhouse had such a cruel master that 61 of the residents committed crimes because they felt it would be better off in the jail than the poorhouse.

Many poorhouses required the "inmates," as to wear uniforms, which many thought was degrading since there was a stigma attached to being in the poorhouse. They were also given other draconian rules to follow. For punishment, usually residents would lose their next meal. But punishments could be harsher and in some cases pillories and stocks were used.

Many people have only known about the poorhouse from Dickens books such as Oliver Twist, or the Community Chest card in the game Monopoly where it says, "Go to Poorhouse! Lose a Turn!" But as more and more people become interested in genealogy, the stories of their relatives in the poorhouse have been researched and become more common knowledge.

Most poorhouses had a "Poor House Cemetery," or something similar, where deceased indigents not claimed by their relatives were buried. These cemetery records are often sought by genealogists. (As time went on, many poorhouses sold their unclaimed bodies to medical schools.) The place where indigents were buried was often called "potter's fields," a sobriquet from the Bible.

Later on, the indigent population of an area was often moved out of the city limits into the rural areas, where the "Poor Farm" concept developed. Instead of breaking rocks or domestic work, male and female residents would do farm labor. Farms could sell the produce they grew to offset their costs. And the residents had fresh food.

There was some good in the poorhouse world other than getting homeless people out of the elements and feeding them. In Maine, for instance, it was documented that many elderly people would close their homes in the winter and move into the poorhouse to save on heat and for companionship with the other residents. Many poorhouses fostered an appealing sense of community. Some even allowed residents to drink beer, although hard liquor was usually not allowed.

Because it was often thought that indigents were taking advantage of the system, wintering in the poorhouse helped begin the practice of having people take an oath swearing that they were indigent and had no other resources before being given assistance.

After a while, poorhouse conditions improved, as residents were given better food and books or magazines to read. There were also occasional outings to museums or movies, and other activities to engage the residents.

The types of patients housed in the poorhouse system varied. Many institutions had a separate building, insensitively called the "Crazy House," to lodge insane inmates. Some had a "Pesthouse," where people with contagious diseases would be housed. There was often a morgue, and a separate building where coffins were stored.

While at first insane people were put into the poorhouse and separated from the rest of the population, after a while Michigan developed a state asylum system for housing the insane. Insane Asylums/Hospitals were in Kalamazoo, Pontiac, Traverse City, and Detroit.

There were a number of circumstances that could have a person assigned to the poorhouse. The reasons for inmates being housed in the Onondaga County Poor House of New York State in 1877 were as follows:

Vagrancy 127
Intemperance direct (alcoholic) 64
Indigent and destitute 53

Lunacy 42
Sickness 30
Debauchery 13
Old Age 10
Bastardy (unwed mother) 7
Lameness 6
Idiocy 6
Blindness 4

For wandering vagrants, there was another alternative: a "tramp house." These would be small buildings, little more than shacks, usually stocked with firewood and mattresses. These tramp houses weren't advertised since most municipalities didn't want to publicize their charity toward tramps. They didn't want to think that their community took it easy on them.

In most cases there are few records of the individual poor farms and poorhouses—it was customary to destroy the records every few years to protect the indigent's privacy. Most information of the individual county farms comes from the state, not the original source. Most poorhouses in Michigan were located in or near the county seat.

Because of the stigma attached to the Poor Farm, in Liverpool, England for instance, when a child was born in the poorhouse, they would put the phony address of 144A Brownhill on their birth certificate to save them the stigma of having others know they were born in a poorhouse.

There was originally a distinction between "poor" and a "pauper" in early England. Someone who was poor was unable to help it and a pauper was someone who was poor because they were unwilling to work. By the time the term was used in 18th-Century America, there was usually no distinction between someone who was poor and someone who was a pauper.

In Michigan, the Poorhouse concept changed when the State of Michigan passed *Public Act 280* in 1939. The act changed the direction of Poor Farms and Poorhouses to an infirmary system, primarily to provide medical and nursing care to the needy.

Photos used are public domain, from Wikipedia, credited, or by the author. If you think you might own the rights to an unaccredited photo, please contact us. We also welcome submissions of pictures and stories.

The Michigan poorhouse pictures are captioned thusly. Other poorhouse photos are basically allegorical, and illustrative of life in a poorhouse. Michigan photos make up the vast majority of the photos and while it would be desirable to have photos of each county's facility, most have few or no pictures at all readily available. The fact that any cameras of the residents would have been seized to help pay any remaining debts of the resident is one of the reasons why.

When titling the chapters I used the name most often used for the institution, such as Eaton County Poor Farm or Cheboygan County Poor Farm Infirmary. Sometimes the facility would almost equally be known by two or more different names—in these cases I've noted this with both names, such as Kent County Poor Farm/County Home.

Poorhouse residents

CHAPTER ONE

Alcona County Poor Farm

Alcona County was set aside in 1840 as "Negwegon County," for a Chippewa Chief. It was renamed Alcona County in 1843. This was a name created by Henry Rowe Schoolcraft, who was a U.S. Indian Agent, and Michigan scholar and author. He made up the county names of Alcona, Algoma, Allegan, Alpena, Arenac, Iosco, Kalkaska, Leelanau, Lenawee, Oscoda and Tuscola by using a combination of Indian, Latin, Greek, and Arabic syllables.

Harrisville Township drew up a charter in 1860 and the rest of the county established a government in 1869.

On May 8, 1877, the Alcona County Board of Supervisors voted to acquire 120 to 200 acres to be used as housing for the poor. They purchased a frame house and farm at a cost of $6,300. The farm was situated in Harrisville Township, and had 200 acres, with 100 acres of improvements. The road it was on was (and still is) named Poor Farm Road.

An 1881 inspection revealed that there was no place at the farm to bathe, other than pails and tubs. The main house was heated by three wood stoves, with adequate ventilation. Food was fresh and nutritious, and the paupers were reportedly happy and satisfied with the care given them. If sick, the doctors provided excellent care and were paid for per visit by the county.

The men and women had separate dormitory facilities but were together during the day, including meals.

There were no facilities for the insane or "idiotic" other than "common rooms." A rear room was finished off to be used as a medical facility. The children went to a school a mile and a half away.

In 1890 the Alcona County Poor Farm had a fire and the main building burned down. Everything in the house and cellar were saved, but there was no insurance on the building.

A 1910 U.S. Census report shows that Alcona County only had 8 indigents, 6 men and 2 women. By 1919 the number had grown to 10 but by 1922 they were down to 5 residents. In 1927 there were 9, and by the 1930s the numbers rose again. In 1931 there were 18 residents and in 1933 there were 21. After the worst of the Great Depression the number fell again—in 1937 they were down to 11.

A 1936 report cites the Poor Farm as "unfit" and their infirmary as "entirely unfit." Both facilities were eventually phased out.

CHAPTER TWO

Alger County Poorhouse

Alger County didn't come into being until 1888, when it was broken off from Schoolcraft County. Alger County contains the Pictured Rocks. Much of their Poorhouse history is lost as there doesn't appear to be much in the way of records.

Since the population of Alger County has always been small (the population is still under 10,000 in 2019), most indigent people were taken care of by their families. There was also the indentured servitude method of auctioning the indigent to the lowest bidder, a method often utilized, especially if there were only one or two indigents in the county. Many of the poor folk were sent to the Schoolcraft County Poor Farm.

In 1919 the Poorhouse had 26 inmates, all men. In 1922 there were 31 men and one woman, in 1924 there were 34 men and still only one woman. In 1925 there were 23 men and no women, and in 1928, there were 43 men and still no women. As the years of the Great Depression dawned, like most poorhouses, the population multiplied. In 1930 the Poorhouse had 67 poor souls, with five of them women. In 1931 the number rose to 100, including 5 women. By 1936 the numbers fell to 76 men and four women.

A 1936 report cites the structure for being a "fire trap," with inadequate means of escape in case of fire. Not long after, the Alger County Poor Farm was phased out, with Social Security and other social services as the main reason.

Alger County Poor Farm/Infirmary Building

CHAPTER THREE

Allegan County Infirmary

The poorhouses of Michigan were referred to in various ways. Allegan County called theirs an "infirmary." Although an infirmary is usually defined as "a place in a large institution for the care of those who are ill," many of the people interred in the infirmary were merely destitute, not ill.

Allegan County was incorporated in 1833 and appointed Giles Scott and H.C. White as the first Overseers of the Poor. A fund was endowed in 1837 for $100 a year, to be used for the care of the poor. The endowment was funded by a "poor tax" charged to the citizenry and provided reimbursement to families taking an indigent into their home.

Although the County Board of Supervisors *approved* buying a farm in 1849, it wasn't until 1866 that the county purchased the J.P. Pope Farm for $7,000, with the intent to use it as a Poor Farm.

In 1869, a second poorhouse was built on the site, a brick, 3-story building. A partially above-ground basement contained the kitchen and dining room. In 1870 the original building was torn down. Next, an insane asylum was added to the complex in 1876. It was a "hospital-style" type of building with 20 rooms. In 1898, a juvenile home was added to house "insane children" separate from the adult insane asylum. In 1899 a hospital "for the isolation of contagious persons" and a telephone was installed at the same time.

The flaws of the institution included no elevators, causing partially lame paupers to have to climb a lot of stairs. The heating plant was expensive to maintain, and often didn't give an adequate amount of heat—especially when cold winds would course through the facility.

The farm was where "undesirables" were sent, as well as serving as a debtor's prison, and an asylum. It also included a home for the disabled and indigent inhabitants of the community from 1866 to 1914.

In 1910 a U.S. report put the population of the poorhouse at 68, with 49 men and 19 women. In 1914 the poor housing was razed and rebuilt, and the records destroyed in the process. In 1921 the facility had 45 men and 14 women. The number stayed steady; in 1925 the number was 46 men and 12 women.

By the Great Depression in 1930, the number had risen to 72 men and 18 women. In 1936 an inspection report said that the present facility was overcrowded at 98 men and 30 women. In 1938 it continued to be overcrowded, with 103 men and 34 women. The facility was eventually phased out as other social programs to assist the poor came into being.

Allegan County Poor Farm/Infirmary

The site of the Poor House Cemetery has a marker that reads:
In Memory of our Departed Friends—1914

The main house was brick, two and a half stories high, 40 by 75 feet, and had a stone basement which contained the inmate's dining room, the kitchen, and the pantry. The ceilings were high and well-lighted. The front rooms on the first and second floor were used by the Keeper and were carpeted, as were the female's bedrooms.

Two bathrooms with bathing facilities were located on the first floor. At first heated by wood stoves, the building had switched to steam heat by 1900.

The facility had a few "mildly insane" patients; there was a separate building where they were housed, along with a few "idiotic" inmates. They were allowed to mingle with the rest of the population during the day and had meals at the same time as the rest of the inmates.

Children were sent to the State Public School and adopted out when possible.

Sleeping and dining quarters in poorhouses were often crowded.

CHAPTER FOUR

Alpena County Poor Farm

Alpena County Poor Farm

On May 16, 1868, the County of Alpena voted to purchase land in Harrisville in the township of Alpena for $5,000, for the purpose of erecting a poor farm, to be paid for by a $1,000 per year tax until paid off.

An 1881 report stated that the house was heated by wood stoves and bathing was in tubs and pails. It was also reported to be not well thought-out to be a poor farm and to have poor ventilation. There were no accommodations for the insane.

In 1891 there was a fire at the Alpena Co. Poor Farm resulting in $2000 damage.

On the bright side, the residents were well-fed and had good clothing. The sick residents were well-taken care of, and the caretakers were very kind to the residents. The district school was a half-mile from the Poorhouse.

The 1910 census report shows that there were 25 people in the county's custody, 21 men and 4 women. Some of the census numbers in the following years included 26 men and 8 women in 1920 and in 1923 there were 29 men and 5 women. The Great Depression year of 1930 saw a decrease, at 22 men and five women, and 1933 saw a small increase to 34 men and five women.

In a 1936 report from the Michigan Welfare Department, when the farm had 30 men and five women, Alpena's Poor Farm was praised for its cleanliness.

CHAPTER FIVE

Antrim County Infirmary

Antrim County did what most counties at first did, and that was to give their paupers aid in the way of food, money, etc. In 1868 it was decided that a domicile for the poor was needed, so the Antrim County Board of Supervisors appointed a committee to investigate it and they located and purchased 90 acres in Torch Lake Township in 1869. A dwelling was built and opened in 1871. The Poorhouse was in Torch Lake Township from 1871 to 1886.

A new Poorhouse, now called the Infirmary, was built in 1889—a two-story, 20 by 80-foot structure, with a 20 by 20-foot, one-story kitchen in the rear of the building. It was heated by a furnace and bathrooms were provided, although a bathing area was needed. It was also cited as needing better drainage, a good supply of water, and fire escapes.

There were two wing extensions at right angles to the main building, one for males and the other females. The wings were two-story, 28-foot structures. An 8-foot basement was under the main building. The facility was built to comfortably house 40 residents and was in Kearney Township, a mile south of Bellaire, off M-88.

The farm raised its own meat and vegetables. In 1902 a new barn was built and carried the label of "Meadowbrook Farm." The name stuck and when the facility became a hospital, it was given the name Meadow Brook Medical Care Facility.

Meadowbrook Farm barn built in 1902

A 1910 U.S. Census report shows 18 men and two women under the county's care. In 1920 this went down to 12 men and five women, and in 1925 the numbers were 16 men and two women. In the Depression year of 1930, there were 29 men and 12 women. In 1936 there were 31 men and eight women.

Antrim County Infirmary farm buildings

Antrim County Infirmary main building

In 1926 the main building burned to the ground. The 23 men and eight women residents were temporarily housed at the Forest Home Township Hall. A new building was constructed in 1927 at the cost of $39, 496. In 1939 the focus of the Infirmary began to be medical care and it operated until 1948, when the facility was renamed the Meadow Brook Hospital.

The hospital did not stop raising poultry and livestock on the property until 1957. In 1968 the original building was repurposed into a long-term nursing facility. In 1983 it became housing units for the elderly. Now called the Meadow Brook Long-Term Care Facility, it is still in business as of 2019.

CHAPTER SIX

Arenac County Farm

Arenac County didn't have a poor house until later than the other county's poorhouses since it wasn't separated from Bay County and organized as a new county until 1883. As late as 1935 Arenac County is listed in state records as having "No infirmary."

The third-smallest Michigan county, Arenac County is on Saginaw Bay, west of the Thumb. Early on, the counties that didn't have a dwelling for the poor would auction them off to the lowest bidder, to be used for labor however the winning bidder deemed fit—as long as they continued to provide food, clothing, and shelter.

A large part of the county is land belonging to the Chippewa and is home to the Chippewa-owned Saganing Eagles Landing Casino.

However, at some point the county did have a poor facility, because in a 1936 State of Michigan report the County Farm was deemed "unfit for human habitation" and was ordered to be closed, which it is assumed it was since no history appears to remain past then.

CHAPTER SEVEN

Baraga County Almshouse/ Poor Farm

The county poorhouse of Baraga County, in Herman, Michigan, in the Upper Peninsula, was often referred to, in the State of Michigan records, by the Old English term of "almshouse," instead of "poorhouse." Interestingly, even though the records refer to it more often as the Baraga County Almshouse, it was located on Poor Farm Road.

One of Michigan's smallest counties, in 2010 the population was less than 9,000 people. Even with a small population, the county still had six indigents in 1910.

A 1907 report from the Michigan State Board of Corrections and Charities stated that the Infirmary was three and a half miles from L'anse, the county seat. It also stated that "The little farm is in the heart of the forest and the building is a two story frame with capacity for twenty inmates; is heated with stoves; has good water supply and sewerage; is planned to secure separation of sexes."

A 1919 report gives the number of the people in the almshouse as 13 men, and by 1925 the number had grown to 20 men. In the Depression year of 1930 there were 29 men (and still no women). In 1934 the number of men went down to 23 and in 1938 it was 12 men. Women were *never* mentioned as tenants of the almshouse—it must have made the separation of the sexes a lot easier.

A 1936 report chastised the house for being overcrowded in the wintertime, although in the September 1936 state inspection there were only 16 men listed, far under the Depression-era high of 29 men.

Baraga County Poor Farm

Baraga County Poor Farm and residents

CHAPTER EIGHT

Barry County Poor Farm

Nothing remains of the Barry County Poor Farm today but the cemetery. Unlike most Poor Farm Cemeteries, this one has grave markers denoting the first and last names of the indigents, along with their birth and death years. Referred to as the Potter's Field Cemetery and also as the Barry County Poor Farm Cemetery, it is located on Nashville Road in Barry County.

In 1849, there was a report in the Michigan Legislative Reports that Barry County didn't have a Poor Farm, but in 1855 the question of a poor farm for the county finally came up and a committee was appointed, and land was found. The Board of Supervisors decided to employ a Superintendent of the Poor to be in charge of the Poor Farm and pay him $800 a year.

By 1856 a Poor Farm had been erected about three and a half miles from Hastings. By 1910 the farm had 44 residents. It was in the north-central portion of Coldwater Township (section 9) and had a house, barn, and other farm buildings, sitting on 140 acres. The farm was administered at first by the "Directors of the Poor," They were later referred to as "Overseers of the Poor."

Most of the resident's food was raised on the farm. A herd of Jersey and Durham cows provided milk and butter. The farm would make $6,000 to $12,000 profit per year from sale of their farm products.

The original Poorhouse was constructed of bricks with two stories and a basement. It was further described as a "long and low structure." The bathroom was in the basement and had warm and cold running water. Heat was by two hot-air furnaces and the house had good ventilation. The paupers were well-fed and well taken care of when ill. The insane were sent to one of the four state asylums.

The main administration building was built in 1881 and was a three-story brick dwelling with forty rooms. It was a well-regarded facility, considered convenient and functional. The grounds were beautiful. The main building contained the Superintendent's Office and the Keeper's private quarters.

The first floor contained the resident's dining rooms, the sitting room, and a large kitchen and pantry area. There was a large room with six beds. This was for the elderly ladies that had trouble navigating the stairs to the second floor to sleep. The second and third floors were designed as dormitories for the residents. The basement was used for storage and contained a bathing area with hot and cold running water.

The dwelling had three fire escapes. The power house provided electricity, the laundry had all modern machinery and the facility had its own water plant and sewers. The buildings were all steam-heated with two hot-air furnaces. The house had good ventilation.

Other buildings on the grounds included a power house, laundry, vegetable cellar, and the hospital. Residents were regularly given medical check-ups and fed good, wholesome food. They were clothed according to the weather and given iron beds with good springs, mattresses, with plenty of blankets and bedding materials.

Able-bodied paupers were provided with work that they were able to perform, monthly devotional services were provided, and holidays observed.

Barry County Poor Farm Cemetery, aka Potter's Field Cemetery.

In 1918 a scuffle at the Poor Farm was reported. LeRoy White hit George Coe, who was in a wheelchair because both of his legs had been amputated after his legs froze and were amputated years earlier. White hit him over the head with an iron bar, which Coe snatched and used to hit White back. Inmates separated them and the doctor was summoned. White was sent to the local jail and later committed to the Kalamazoo State Hospital.

In 1920 the population was 37 men and 10 women, and in 1925 there were 42 men and 9 women. By the Depression year of 1930 there were 60 men and 13 women. As the economy improved in 1938, there were 31 men and five women.

In 1925 a destitute farmer hanged himself at the Barry County Poor Farm.

Poor Farm workers

CHAPTER NINE

Bay County Poor Farm

Bay County Poor Farm

The Poor Farm of Bay County was in Essexville, Hampton Township, about four miles from the county seat, Bay City. It was established in 1857. The main building was of frame construction and had two and half stories that housed both paupers and caretakers. There was a separate house for the Keeper. Heating was by wood and coal stoves. The men's quarters were on the first floor of the main building.

The farm was on 120 acres of what was described as "so-so" land. The residents worked on the farm, plowing in the summer and sowing in the autumn, working with the farm animals. The grain grown was stored in one of many outbuildings, about 80 yards from the main house. A small cemetery was established.

There was a bathtub, and residents were required to bathe at least once a week. There were separate quarters and dining rooms for men and women. In 1872 there were 64 paupers living at the house. A report calls the house generally well-kept, with the female quarters much neater than the male's quarters. There was a separate brick building in the back, used to house the "insane and idiotic." Medical care was provided by a doctor who checked on patients at least twice weekly and provided treatment when necessary.

By 1880, a comfortable part of the house, warm and with good ventilation, was set aside as a hospital area.

The meals were adequate and nutritious, and clothing provided included a separate suit for Sundays. Each pauper received attire for everyday wear and a suit to wear to church on Sunday. Children were adopted out, and those not adopted were sent to the State School at Coldwater.

In 1889 the Poor Farm was refurbished, painted throughout, and new hardwood floors were installed. By 1889 the insane were no longer housed at the Poor Farm but sent to the Eastern Asylum at Pontiac.

Crops grown on the 120 acres included, according to an 1889 report, "Wheat, 190 bushels; corn, 800 bushels; oats 750 bushels; peas, 80 bushels; potatoes, 250 bushels; hay, 20 tons; rutabagas and carrots, 1000 bushels; parsnips, onions, beans, 35 bushels; a large quantity of cabbage; milk cows, 7; two spans of horses, colts, etc., pigs old and young—upwards of 40."

In 1905 the old, wood building burned down. The County Supervisors voted to spend $25,000 for a three-story brick building, along with some other farm buildings.

In 1920, the number of residents of Bay County's Poor Farm was 68 men and 15 women. This increased to 77 men and 16 women in 1930, and in 1938 the population included 128 men and 25 women.

In 1930 the Bay County Poor Farm suffered a $30,000 fire which started in a haystack which ignited from sparks from the threshing machine. No one was injured, but two barns and another farm building burned. In 1905 a defective chimney caused a fire which burned down the main house.

A 1936 Michigan report on County Homes reported that the Bay County Home had a jail cell in the basement that was used to restrain violent patients and discipline others. Also, a dog and her puppies resided in the basement. It was said to be, "An old house, hard to keep clean."

In 1964, the Bay County Infirmary/Poor Farm became the Bay County Medical Care Facility.

The Poor Farm itself closed in 1964. The Bay County Poor Farm Cemetery, also known as the County Farm Cemetery, was located at 584 W. Hampton Road in Essexville in Bay County. Most of the site is now underneath the Bay County Golf Course.

Bay County Poor Farm Burial Grounds

Bay County Poor House

CHAPTER TEN

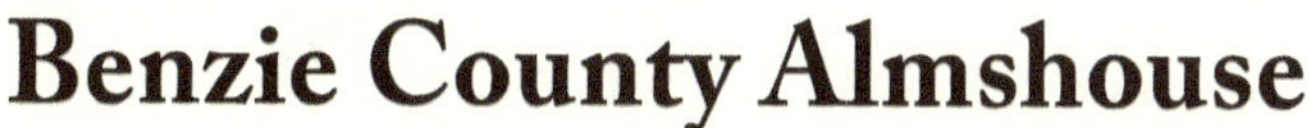

Benzie County Almshouse

Benzie County wasn't set off from surrounding counties until 1863, and then wasn't organized until 1869, partly due to the Civil War. For this reason, they also didn't have an official poorhouse until after all the other counties had them.

Benzie County is on Lake Michigan in the Lower Peninsula. It is west of Traverse City and contains portions of the Pere Marquette State Forest and the Sleeping Bear Dunes. Benzie has the smallest land area of Michigan's 83 counties. It was organized in 1869, with Beulah as the county seat. The Betsie River runs through it and a derivation of the name is where the county name of Benzie came from.

Michigan records list the poorhouse facility as the "Benzie County Almshouse," and other records are few. In an official census of Michigan Poorhouses and Farms in 1910, Benzie County isn't listed.

In the 1919 State of Michigan reports, Benzie County Almshouse is listed as having 18 men and three women. In 1925 the census was still 18 men, and there were four women. In 1929 the numbers were 14 men and four women. As the Depression started, in 1930 there were 18 men and five women in the almshouse.

In 1933 there were 25 men and eleven women; in 1938 there were 14 men and 11 women. The almshouse was eventually phased out, although records are scarce as to exactly when.

CHAPTER ELEVEN

Berrien County Poor Farm/Infirmary

The subject of a Poor Farm for Berrien County was first discussed on October 27, 1837 by the Berrien County Board of Supervisors, not long after Michigan statehood. But the first action to help the poor didn't occur until 1847 when land was purchased in Berrien Township for the building of a County Poor Farm.

Berrien County Infirmary/Poor Farm

First discussed in 1837, a brick, two-story poorhouse with a large wing was built in 1847 for $200 and a farm of 160 acres, 50 already cultivated, was purchased for $1,220.

In 1868 a fire started in the kitchen and destroyed the main building. The 35 residents were housed in a building rented for them in Berrien. Through 1869 the new county home was built, opening in 1870. Made of brick, it was much more fireproof. The farm buildings that burned in the fire were also replaced.

In 1910 the Berrien County Poorhouse, in Berrien Center, housed 58 residents, 31 men and 27 women. Charles Miller was appointed three times to be the Superintendent of the Poor and was succeeded by Chester Badger. A report that year said that the "building was in good condition and the paupers well-cared for."

In 1920 there were 41 men and 27 women; in 1925 there were 77 men and 20 women and in the Depression year of 1930 there were 104 men and 36 women. By 1935 there were 153 men and 52 women. In 1938 there were 152 men and 48 women.

In 1928 a new $50,000 addition was built to house the mentally insane and the mentally ill. In 1937 another new structure was built and named the Berrien County Hospital and Infirmary. This became the Berrien General Hospital Center, and then was most recently renamed the Lakeland Medical Center.

The 200-acre complex is today called the Matrix Center and includes a facility for Long Term Care, Love Creek Nature Park, the Berrien County Juvenile Center, and the County Dog Pound.

The Berrien County Poor Farm Cemetery, also known as the County Infirmary Cemetery, is in Berrien Springs in the back of the original 200 acres. It is no longer distinctly marked and is classified as "abandoned" in county records. Burials have been dug up while building other structures in the area. However, there is one area that is known as the County Infirmary Cemetery. It is known to be cemetery grounds due to the sunken ground and pieces of headstones that remain on the site.

Overview of the Berrien County Infirmary Cemetery

CHAPTER TWELVE

Branch County Infirmary

Branch County is located on the Michigan-Indiana state border. Coldwater is within the county, the site of the State School of Michigan, later known as the Coldwater State Home and Training School.

The Branch County Infirmary was completed in October 1847 and cost $500 to build. A hundred and sixty acres were purchased, 35 of which were improved. The brick building had two stories, a good water supply, and good drainage.

The 1910 Census reported that there were 52 people at the infirmary, located about two miles from Coldwater, Michigan, with 27 men and 25 women. In 1920 there were 37 men and ten women. In 1925 there were 35 men and 27 women, and in 1930, 44 men and 23 women. The numbers held steady in 1938 with 42 men and 24 women.

A 1936 inspection report states that the infirmary lacked adequate fire protection, and lacked a safe exit from the building in case of fire. It wasn't long after that the infirmary no longer housed paupers as they were taken care of by Social Security and other new social services.

CHAPTER THIRTEEN

Calhoun County Almshouse/Infirmary

Calhoun County Poor Facilities

In 1846 the county commissioners gave notice to the state that they were suspending the Poor Laws canon for Calhoun County.

They had been caring for the indigent without constructing a poorhouse and found this to be more economical for them.

This changed in three years, as in 1849 the Calhoun County Board of Commissioners appointed three Commissioners of the Poor for three-year terms. They then purchased the land that was the northwest one-quarter, section 9, in the township of Marengo, about two miles from Marshall.

From 1850 to 1851 a wooden poorhouse structure was built. Additions were made over time, and by 1876 the facility consisted of a main building that was a two-story, 110 by 30 feet structure, with a brick wing to the north that had one-story with a basement.

The first-story portion was used to house the insane. The basement portion was used to house the hot-air furnaces that provided the facility's heat. Another wing to the north was two stories, 20 by 30 feet, containing the sitting rooms and bedrooms of the inmates.

The second floor of the main building was the living quarters of the Keeper of the Poor, and the first floor contained the offices for the facility and the main dining room. With the barns and other farm buildings, in 1876 the entire facility was appraised at $18,000. In 1876 they had 50 residents, and 104 had been admitted throughout the following year. In 1910 they had 52 residents, 36 men and 16 women.

In 1920 there were 68 men and 42 women; in 1925 the total was 100 men and 32 women. In the Depression year of 1930 the numbers were up to 162 men and 65 women. In 1935 there were 229 men and 81 women and in 1938 there were *340* men and *110* women!

Children were taken to the State School at Coldwater and in 1876 they took 10, with a total of 25 sent to the State School since the establishment of the facility. Separation of the sexes was practiced. Heat was by steam and the facility had an excellent water supply and a good sewer system.

A brick annex included a boiler house, rooms for the "idiotic and demented," laundry facilities, and bathrooms.

The farm was very productive, and one year was found to have produced, "474 bushels (of) wheat, 200(bushels of) oats, 1,400 bushels (of) corn, 336 (bushels of) potatoes, 15 bushels of apples, 55 bushels (of) garden vegetables, 600 heads (of) cabbage, 24 tons (of) hay, corn fodder from 18 acres, two tons of pork, and 15 and 1/2 acres of wheat on the ground."

A visiting commissioner said about the farm, "few poorhouses as clean, none cleaner." The Infirmary became the Calhoun County Medical Care Facility.

CHAPTER FOURTEEN

Cass County Infirmary

Up until 1852 there was property in Cass County to house the poor, but on it was only a small log cabin, located about three miles from Cassopolis in Jefferson Township. In 1853 the Cass County Board voted to spend $1,200 to build a Poor Farm. In 1871 a new building was erected to house the county's insane—it was called "the asylum." There was also a separate hospital building.

In 1869 the original home was deemed inadequate and a new home was built in 1869 and 1870 for $6,300. The new home was a three-story brick building, with a two-story brick annex. Heat was by steam.

The farm consists of 280 acres. In 1871 a new, two-story building to house the insane was erected. The thrifty board was glad when the entire project was completed for under $15,000.

In 1900 the U.S. Census reported 59 residents of the Poor Farm. In 1910 there were 30 residents of the infirmary located in Cassopolis. This included 20 men and 10 women. Early inspection reports mention the lack of fire escapes, and that new floors were needed in some of the rooms.

In 1901, Frank Bailey, a dwarf, avoided being assigned to the County Infirmary. He began using his "talking machine" to try to raise money to get his dwarf wife out of the poor facility. There were unfortunately no more details given about the "talking machine" in the news accounts. Bailey was later found starving in his home and successfully sent to the Infirmary where his wife was.

In 1933, the staff walked out in support of the old caretakers who were fired, leaving the new caretakers without a staff. Although news accounts don't seem to give a date when they all returned, they probably did at some point because in 1936 the Cass County Infirmary was given good grades by the Michigan Welfare Department inspections.

CHAPTER FIFTEEN

Charlevoix County Infirmary

Charlevoix County was first set off by surveyors between 1840 and 1841. The original name was Keskkauko and was changed to Charlevoix in 1843. With changing boundaries throughout the 1840s and 1850s, Charlevoix became just a township. It then regained its county status, and the county seat was East Jordan. The Infirmary was in Ironton. A 1910 report described the Ironton Poorhouse/Infirmary as a small frame building with few conveniences. But that was okay, since there were very few paupers in the area then, concluded the report.

Therefore, the Charlevoix County Infirmary, the county's choice for the name of its poorhouse, was organized later than other poorhouses. It was in South Arm, which combined with East Jordan in 1878. It stayed there even after the county seat was moved to the City of Charlevoix and then was relocated in 1900.

The Charlevoix County Infirmary had 9 residents in 1900. In 1910 they had 12 residents—8 men and 4 women. In 1920 there were 19 men and two women. In 1925 there were 24 men and five women; in 1930 there 44 men and 10 women. In 1938 there were 47 men and four women. When they died most of the Infirmary residents were buried in the Sunset Hill Cemetery in East Jordan.

The 1936 Michigan Welfare Department declared that the facility was well-run. The area that the Infirmary was on is now the Grandvue Medical Care facility.

Grandvue Medical Care Facility in East Jordan, Michigan

CHAPTER SIXTEEN

Cheboygan County Poor Infirmary

Cheboygan County started as a Chippewa Indian settlement. Settlers from down south moved in around 1844 and established the Village of Duncan. It was at first the county seat, and then in 1870 the City of Cheboygan was made the county seat.

It was a while before the county merited a poorhouse, but finally the Poor Infirmary, as they called it, was built about three miles from Cheboygan. It was a wood, two-story building with a heating plant installed. It was originally a mill boarding house. It had bathrooms, steam heat, and a good water supply and drainage.

In 1907, in the Biennial Report of the State Board of Corrections and Charities for Michigan, it was stated that the house was too small, the bathing accommodations were inadequate, and it was difficult to care for in its crowded condition. It was recommended the house be enlarged and remodeled.

The Cheboygan County Poor Infirmary had 19 patients in 1910, 16 were men and 3 were women. The number grew to 34 men and nine women in 1920 and to 40 men and six women in 1925. In 1938 the count was 38 men and 10 women.

By 1950 the Infirmary had closed, and the county sold the building and land to help fund the "Northern Michigan Fair" held in Cheboygan County.

CHAPTER SEVENTEEN

Chippewa County Poor Farm

Chippewa County was organized in 1826 with Sault Ste. Marie as its county seat. It is in the Upper Peninsula and is the second-largest county by land area. It has parts of two Native American reservations within its borders.

In 1907 the Poor Farm main building had a fire and was completely destroyed. All the residents escaped injury. The house was rebuilt as a two-story frame building and was about four miles from Ste. Sault Marie. There were bathroom facilities with a good water supply and drainage.

However, one report mentions that it had poor ventilation, and was heated by stoves. It also needed to install fire escapes. Regardless, the farm soon housed 21 paupers—16 men and 5 women.

In 1920 the Poor Farm had nine men and nine women. By 1925 there were 27 men and six women. In 1930 there were 44 men and four women, and in 1938 there were 46 men and seven women.

CHAPTER EIGHTEEN

Clare County Poor Farm/Infirmary

Clare County Infirmary

In 1871 the first Clare County Poor Farm was built on 80 acres in Section 35 of Grant Township. When in 1879 the decision to move the county seat to Harrison was made, the Poor Farm was moved there also. The new facility was on 120 acres in Section 20 of Hayes Township.

In 1910 the Clare County Infirmary was within the village limits of Harrison and had 9 residents, all of them men. The infirmary was a two-story frame building and had been remodeled and added to. An 1896 report says that it was in good condition and had bathing, bathroom and sewer facilities. Heat was via wood stoves, and the sick were attended to by good, competent doctors and nurses.

The residents were given, according to the report, "Good, substantial food and plenty of it, and clothing suitable for the seasons." Insane persons were sent to the Northern Asylum of Traverse City.

In 1912 the Poor Farm was renamed the Clare County Infirmary and was moved to County Farm Road near Harrison.

There were ten men and three women in 1920 and in 1925 there were 25 men and one woman. The Depression year of 1930 brought 23 men and three women to the Infirmary. In 1935 there were 19 men and four women, and in 1938 there were 16 men and nine women.

One of the few newspaper articles about the facility occurred when a resident choked to death on an apple in 1931. The Michigan Welfare Department declared in 1936 that they were one of the better facilities.

The Clare County Infirmary

The third facility on County Farm Road in Harrison was used until 1945 when it was closed. The building burned down in 1948.

CHAPTER NINETEEN

Clinton County Poorhouse

In 1839 the Clinton County Board of Commissioners appointed three men to be "County Superintendents of the Poor." In 1844 the first motions to purchase land for the construction of a poorhouse was made, and in November of 1944 the township purchased a tract which was located, according to the deed, at "township 5 north, range 2 west (De Witt), the northwest quarter of the southwest quarter and the west half of the south fraction of the northwest quarter of section 9." The county paid $661.68 for the property but never built on it.

Finally, a farm in St. Johns was purchased in 1867 for $3,500. It contained 76 acres, forty under cultivation, and an orchard of 175 fruit trees. A poorhouse was erected in 1871 and another building was added in 1879. In 1879 there were 30 paupers housed in the poorhouse.

According to an 1896 report, the main house had bath and bathroom facilities, was heated by a furnace and stoves, and ventilation was fair. The insane were housed in a different building and the paupers were receiving excellent care—food, clothing, and care of the sick.

It was estimated in 1879 that the crop output for that year yielded $793.30. The total Poor Farm expenses for the year were recorded as $3,816.23 and the total value of the poor-farm and appurtenances were given as $8,056.50.

According to the 1910 U.S. Census, the Clinton County Poorhouse in St. Johns had 32 residents—17 men and 15 women. In 1920 there were 36 men and one woman and in 1925 there were 29 men and 14 women. In 1930 there were 37 men and 14 women; in 1938 there were 42 men and 17 women.

In a state report in 1936, the Clinton County Poorhouse was reported to be overcrowded—it was designed for 40 residents but instead housed 40 men and 16 women—56 in all.

The Clinton County Poorhouse was reported to have padlocked cells, where residents were put as punishment, with only bread and water rations. The poorhouse was eventually phased out.

CHAPTER TWENTY

The Crawford County Infirmary

Located in the center of the upper portion of Michigan's Lower Peninsula, Crawford County's county seat is Grayling, a large hunting and camping area, which is where the County Infirmary was located. It was founded in 1840 as "Shawono County," and in 1843 was renamed Crawford County for a Revolutionary War hero.

An 1896 report said that the Crawford County Poorhouse and other buildings were in good condition. The facility had tubs for bathing and was heated with wood stoves. A physician was hired to regularly look after them and nursing care was provided when needed. The residents were fed well and adequately clothed for the season.

The institution had no insane or idiotic residents so there weren't separate places built for them. There were no children living there in 1896 but there was an excellent school within four blocks of the house in case any ever did. (They didn't.)

According to a 1910 report, the Crawford County Infirmary in Grayling had six inmates—all were men. In 1920 there were nine men and no women; in 1925 the count was 15 men and nine women. In 1930 there were 12 men and three women and in 1938 there were 12 men and once again no women.

Probably the most shocking development occurrence happened in 1931 when a former inmate killed the infirmary Superintendent and two others! He was sentenced to and died in the electric chair in Arkansas.

CHAPTER TWENTY-ONE

Delta County Almshouse/ Infirmary

An 1896 report judged the almshouse to be in good condition. It was in the township of Wells and contained a bathroom with tub and hot and cold water. Heat was by wood stoves with good ventilation. The hospital was in a separate building and was in good shape, heated by steam, and lit by gas. No accommodations were provided for the insane and idiotic because there weren't any. A school was close by.

In 1910 the Delta County Almshouse in Escanaba had 36 inmates—30 men and 5 women. In 1920 there were 77 men and five women and in 1925 there were 81 men and four women. In 1930 the count ballooned to 94 men and three women. In 1938 there were 180 men and no women.

In 1930 one of the residents was convicted of manslaughter after getting into a fight with and killing one of the other inmates.

In 1930 a new wing was added to the almshouse, however, in a 1936 report, the facility was judged to be overcrowded and lacking adequate fire protection and fire exits. It was eventually phased out.

CHAPTER TWENTY-TWO

Dickinson County Poorhouse

The newest of Michigan's counties, in 1891 Dickinson County was formed from parts of Iron, Marquette, and Menominee Counties. It is in the Upper Peninsula and was named for David Dickinson, a Detroit lawyer who served as U.S. Postmaster General in President Grover Cleveland's Cabinet from 1888 to 1889.

Although Dickinson County had a Poorhouse, records are scanty. The poorhouse was in the City of Iron Mountain. In 1917 a major fire struck the facility. Starting in the kitchen, the fire spread and destroyed the main house, the hospital, the ice house, and the root cellar. All the patients made it out safely.

According to state reports from the Michigan Reports of the Superintendents of the Poor, Dickinson County usually had about 20 to 35 people housed in the facility in the 1920s. In 1925 there were 26 men and three women. In the 1930s, the number went up to 65 to 75 inmates and in 1938 there were 60 men and five women.

In 1936 the Michigan Department of Welfare complimented the Dickinson County Poorhouse, calling it well-maintained, and the patients well taken care of.

CHAPTER TWENTY-THREE

Eaton County Poor Farm

The Eaton County Poor Farm was in the Township of Chester, three miles west of the county seat, Charlotte. According to an 1896 report, it was heated by steam, well-ventilated, and had a bathroom with a bathtub. The inhabitants were treated humanely and "no corporeal punishment was allowed." (Stories abound of paupers being whipped and beaten in some facilities.) It was mentioned that some of the "more intelligent" residents helped the medical staff.

There were no separate facilities for the idiotic and insane since there officially weren't any. The district school was close by.

A 1910 report said that the Eaton County Poor Farm in Charlotte had 31 inmates—19 men and 12 women. In 1920 there were 33 men and eight women. In 1925 there were 40 men and 15 women, and in 1930 there were 38 men and 20 women. In 1938 there were 50 men and 19 women living at the Poor Farm.

Experiments on soil and wheat growth were conducted at the Poor Farm in 1919. It was determined that acid phosphate, manure, and lime made the best fertilizer for the growing of wheat.

In 1930 an inspection at the County Poor Farm revealed that the residents were being fed spoiled meat, were mistreated and "manhandled" by the staff, and the facility was not kept clean, especially one annex, which was "unfit for human habitation." It was stated that the Keeper had hit and slapped many residents. The Cook also struck the young women under her charge.

In 1936 an inspection reported that the Poor Farm was overcrowded and lacked adequate laundry, kitchen, and bathroom facilities. The nursing care was also judged inadequate. This was around the time when many poor houses were closing due to the safety nets of Social Security and other funds—but not Eaton County's! The Eaton County Poor Farm wasn't phased out until 1966 and the residents sent to the then-new Eaton County Medical Care Facility.

Eaton County Poor Farm

CHAPTER TWENTY-FOUR

Emmet County Poorhouse

In 1896 a state of Michigan report on poorhouses, it was reported that the paupers were treated like family in the Emmet County Poorhouse. The food was good, wholesome, and plain. Heat was by wood stove and ventilation was from doors and windows. Cotton and woolen clothing were provided, as the occasion warranted. There were no idiotic, insane, or children in the Poorhouse so no accommodations for them were needed.

In 1910 the Emmet County Poorhouse, in the Township of Maple Rivers in Alanson, had two residents—one man and one woman. The 1910 report goes on to state that the poorhouse was about twelve miles from Petoskey. It was a two-story, frame structure, and said to be fairly arranged. However, there were no bathing facilities in the house, or sewers, or ventilation.

In 1920, there were 17 men and four women incarcerated in the Poorhouse. In 1925 it was 29 men and five women. The 1930 count was 40 men and 12 women, and in 1938 there were 34 men and 15 women.

CHAPTER TWENTY-FIVE

Genesee County Farm/Infirmary

The County Farm of Genesee County was in Burton Township, about two and a half miles from the City of Flint. Genesee County had purchased one hundred and thirteen acres for $1,250 to build the facility. Twenty of the acres were "improved," or cleared of trees and ready for farming.

The first mention of a poor house in Genesee County was at a meeting on December 5, 1836, when aid was given to a county resident. Before 1839 a distinction was made between a "town poor person" and a "county poor person," the assertion being that each should take care of their own. In 1839 the distinction between a town poor person and a county poor person was changed so that all paupers were considered wards of the county. Eventually, all Michigan counties did the same. A board of superintendents for the poor was appointed. However, it took about ten years before property was purchased and a poorhouse built.

In 1875 the County Farm was said to contain a "wild boy," who had to be chained constantly or he would run into the woods and climb a tree.

An 1896 report states that the Genesee County Farm main building was 16 by 20 feet, brick, and had two stories. The front rooms of the building were occupied by the women, and the rooms to the rear by the men, with a common sitting room and dining room.

Bathing facilities were good, with hot and cold running water and bathtubs available. Women were required to bathe on Fridays, with the men required to bathe and shave on Saturdays. The inmates did light work voluntarily and were fed healthy and substantial food. Each of the inmates was given two suits of good, well-made clothing and were always well-treated.

There wasn't a separate medical building, but a physician checked in with the farm twice a week to check on everyone's general welfare, oftener if necessary. There was a separate dwelling for the "mildly insane," but the "idiotic" were kept with the general population. According to the 1896 report, no favoritism was shown to any of the inmates. There was a district school close by when there were children.

In 1910 the Poor House, was reported to have 67 residents—42 men and 25 women. In 1920 the state records gave the count as 129 men and 39 women. In 1925 there were 105 men and 42 women. In the Depression year of 1930 there were 307 men and 182 women. In 1935 there were 328 men and 161 women and in 1938 there were 723 men and 446 women!

A 1922 article in the Detroit Free Press reports on "awful" conditions at the Poor House, causing a special committee to be appointed to investigate it. Reports included a 90-year-old woman "lying in filth," bedbugs visibly crawling on the walls, and inadequate food rations, which rarely included more than soup and bread without butter. A sugar bowl on the table contained no sugar.

The Poor Farm turned things around, and in 1936 they were cited as one of the better-run poor farms in Michigan. This was determined after a Welfare Department inspection.

The Genesee County Poor House

CHAPTER TWENTY-SIX

Gladwin County Poor Farm/Infirmary

The Gladwin County Poor Farm was in Sage Township, about two miles from the City of Gladwin. It included 165 acres, 65 of which were farmed. An 1896 report states that the main building was in fair condition but that improvements were under consideration. At that time there were no bathing facilities and the building was warmed by stoves.

The 1896 report goes on to praise the Keeper and his wife for their care of the paupers—they are described as "warm and sympathizing." There were no separate quarters for insane or idiotic people since as of then there had been no need. The children went to a nearby district school.

A 1910 report says that there were 14 residents, six men and eight women at that time. In 1920 the numbers were 13 men and three women and in 1930 there were 13 men and four women. In 1938 there were 14 men and two women living at the Poor Farm.

In 1936, it was determined by an investigation into all the state poor facilities of Michigan that the Gladwin County Poor Farm was "unfit for human habitation." It was also cited as a fire trap, and the Gladwin County Infirmary was recommended to be closed at once since "the risk of fire is too great to risk delay." The infirmary was closed but the habitat for the paupers remained open until at least 1939.

CHAPTER TWENTY-SEVEN

Gogebic County Poor House/Infirmary

The Gogebic County Infirmary was in Bessemer in the Upper Peninsula. An 1896 state report gave it poor grades by saying it was in fair condition and the inspectors thought that "we do not make much use of it."

The infirmary did have adequate bathing facilities for the summer months but inadequate in the winter. It was warmed by stoves and had partial ventilation. Despite the physical condition of the pauper's quarters, it was said that the treatment of them was excellent. Food and clothing were good, and the sick were sent to either Union Hospital at Ironwood, or Gogebic Hospital in Bessemer. In the 1896 report they had no idiotic or insane, and children went to a nearby school.

In 1910 the facility had six residents, five men and one woman. In 1920 there were 49 men and one woman, and in 1925 there were 62 men and still only one woman. In 1930 there were two women and 115 men. For 1935 the count was 208 men and five women and in 1938 there were 436 men and 20 women.

In 1935 the county wanted to find a new location for the infirmary because mining operations had damaged the old one. A year later in 1936 the infirmary was cited as being in a well-maintained condition.

Gogebic County Poor House, Bessemer, Michigan (about 1905)

CHAPTER TWENTY-EIGHT

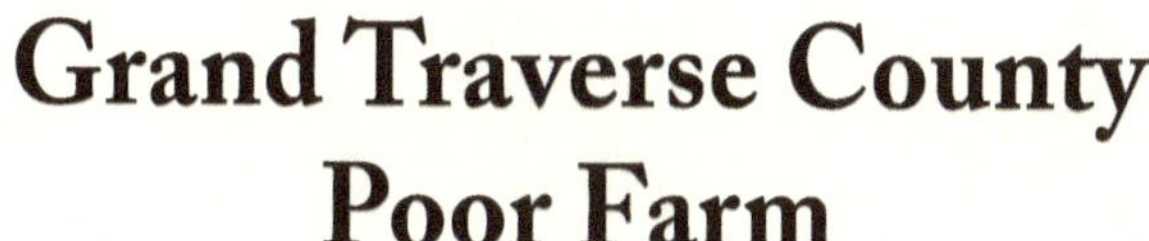

Grand Traverse County Poor Farm

In the 1896 Michigan report on poorhouses, it stated that the Grand Traverse County Poorhouse was within the city limits of Traverse City and in good condition. The Keeper was paid $2.50 per resident each week and he kept the residents well-fed and well-clothed. There were no idiots or insane residents, and children were sent to the public school.

However, by the early 1900s the poorhouse was reportedly considered "one of the worst in the state." It was described as a ramshackle, old two-story house on Boardman Street near the courthouse. In 1906 the Grand Traverse County Board of Supervisors acted by purchasing twenty acres three miles outside of town in Garfield Township, upon which they would have a new Poor Farm erected. But in 1910, when the county still hadn't started construction on the new facility, the state condemned the old poorhouse, prompting quick action.

The state's report stated that the poorhouse building was totally inadequate and vermin infested. In the winter five men were crammed into a bedroom meant for one. The sick room was only five by nine and a half feet large. The report called the poorhouse condition "a most disgraceful blot on the community."

By 1911 the county had built a "handsome, red-brick, two-story building" on Cass Road near the Sabin Dam.

Old House, home of employees and their families of the North Michigan Asylum

In 1920 there were 23 men and two women living in the confines of the home. In 1925 there were 21 men and five women, and in 1930 there were 35 men and nine women. In 1938 the population grew to 126 men and 173 women.

In 1936 the Michigan Welfare Department, in its report, said that the Poor Farm was well-run.

In 1881 Traverse City also became home to an insane asylum/hospital, joining Michigan psychiatric facilities in Pontiac and Kalamazoo. The Traverse City facility was known as the Northern Michigan Asylum, the Traverse City State Hospital, and the Traverse City Regional Psychiatric Hospital.

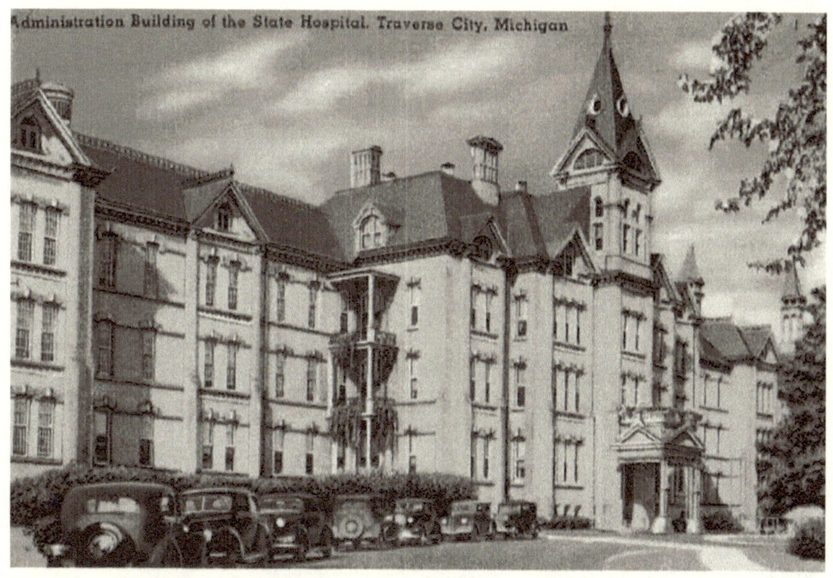

Traverse City State Hospital in 1930

Mentally ill patients from the poorhouse and elsewhere in the area were admitted to the facility, constructed in the "Kirkbride style." This was an architectural style used for mental asylums that emphasized natural light and air circulation. Construction was usually with the "bat wing" style floor plan, with wings springing outward from the main building in the center. Men and women would be housed on opposite sides of the building. The model was popular near the end of the 19th Century and used for mental facilities all over the United States and Canada—there were over 50 built in the style.

Michigan had three asylums built in the Kirkbride style, with the first being the Kalamazoo Regional Psychiatric Hospital in 1858 and the next the Pontiac State Hospital, built in 1878 and then the Traverse City State Hospital in 1885. Later the Kirkbride style of asylums was phased out, mostly because of the immensity of the buildings and the upkeep required.

The Traverse City State Hospital operated from 1885 until the year 2000. The main building is now inactive but still standing. Its administrator was Dr. James Decker Munson, who has a present-day hospital facility named for him. He believed that natural beauty such as in flowers and trees was therapeutic to mental patients and had many botanical items planted on the grounds.

Traverse City State Hospital

The large facility had many outbuildings serving as cottage residences and medical buildings.

Cottage Buildings of Kalamazoo State Hospital

Another view of Traverse City State Hospital

Underground tunnel connecting cottages of the hospital system

In 1948 the facility had a large fire, burning down one of the many cottage residences located on the grounds.

Firefighting at Grand Traverse Poor Farm

CHAPTER TWENTY-NINE

Gratiot County Poor Farm

It was called the Gratiot County Poorhouse, or Almshouse, but the official name was the Gratiot County Poor Farm and in 1914 it was changed to the Gratiot County Infirmary.

It was located about a mile and a half from Ithaca, the county seat, in Newark Township. The main building was two stories high and contained 16 rooms—two sitting rooms, a dining room, a bathroom, 11 bedrooms, and a room for the insane. It was 22 by 50 feet and valued at $7,000. A wing was added, 28 by 30 feet, with two more sitting rooms, a kitchen and pantry, and six bedrooms, used by the females.

An 1896 inspection said that the poor farm was in good condition and the food was described as "plain, good and plentiful."

There was a small room for bathing and tubs were located in there. Heat was provided by wood stoves and the ventilation, something always of concern to the inspectors, was by windows and doors. The paupers received clothing that was adequate for the weather and were fed bread, butter and vegetables. Meat was served three times a day except Sunday, when it was twice a day. Coffee or tea was served twice a day.

Contrary to most poorhouses, Gratiot County's kept detailed records, including federal, state, and Civil War censuses, "cause of pauperism," births and birthdates, marriages, divorces, deaths, adoptions, voter records, land ownership and tax records, criminal and civil court records, biographies, news clippings, and more! Notations were made, such as "lazy" or "took a French leave." A French leave was when they slipped away in the middle of the night without telling anyone.

Some of the "Causes of Pauperism" listed included:

Subject was indigent, homeless, and had no money
Subject was sick, injured, blind, crippled, epileptic, or insane (these patients were usually transferred, as mentioned, to the relevant facility)
A subject's family refuses to care for him or her
The subject had no family or friends
The subject was pregnant and unmarried
The subject had been engaged in prostitution
The subject was an orphaned or abandoned child
Various miscellaneous reasons

Children, if any, were sent to school at the State Public School in Coldwater, unless they could be placed with a local family. Some inmates were sent to the Traverse City State Mental Hospital and some to the Tuscola School for Epileptics, which was in Indianfields Township in Tuscola County, also known as the State School for Epileptics. The sick residents were well-attended to with medical care and nursing.

Transfers were also made to the Michigan School for the Deaf, the Michigan School for the Blind, and also the county jail. Some, especially "wayward" boys or girls, were exiled to their county of residency.

The average number of paupers at a time was 35, mostly men. The year they had the most residents was 1902, with 66 people, next was 1909 with 65. In 1910 it had 34 residents, with 27 men and 7 women. In December 1915, a news article in the Gratiot Herald mentions a drive to buy a gramophone for the Poor Farm. In 1920 there were 42 men and 17 women.

In the 1930s the average number of residents was 73 to 80, in 1938 it was 46, and in 1940 the facility averaged 40 at a time.

In 1936 the Almshouse was cited for inadequate fire protection, as well as not having adequate exits in case of fire.

As Social Security and other safety net programs for the poor came into place, the infirmary was phased out as a place where paupers would live.

Gratiot County Almshouse

CHAPTER THIRTY

Hillsdale County Poorhouse

Hillsdale County Poorhouse

The restored "Will Carleton Poorhouse" is at 200 Wolcott Drive, Hillsdale, MI.

In 1836, Hillsdale County paid $814 for a 160-acre farm, of which 50 acres had been improved. It was located at the intersection of Bacon Street and Spring Street in Cambria. The property's buildings were added to, and this included a "double log house" which cost $250 to construct. Also built was a large frame barn for $180. In 1850 there were 12 paupers, ranging in age from 10 to 80 years old.

In 1853 a poorhouse was built on Wolcott Road, east of the Village of Hillsdale. Fieldstone from the surrounding area was used in its construction. In 1855 a barracks-like structure was built to house the paupers.

In 1867 there was a fire at the Poorhouse, and the Poorhouse was moved to various houses on Short Street, and then to various places on Cambria Street. Built of stone, the original poorhouse's outer walls were rebuilt, and it became a private residence.

The Cambria houses were torn down and a large brick building became the Poorhouse. This building eventually became the Hillsdale County Medical Care Facility and Rehabilitation Center. One of the buildings was divided into apartments. The paupers buried at the back were moved to Lakeview Cemetery.

In 1880 there were 24 residents. One was blind, one was both blind and "idiotic," three were insane, two others were insane and disabled, and six others were disabled. The insane and idiotic had separate apartments.

In an 1896 report, the facilities were described as good, with bath tubs and heated by a furnace and stoves. The paupers were said to be treated "with good and humane treatment," and they were required to "work moderately and keep themselves clean."

Poet Will Carleton's inspiration for the poem "Over the Hill to the Poorhouse" (reproduced at the end of this book) was the Hillsdale County Poorhouse since Carleton was from Hillsdale. Carleton went to Hillsdale College, and every Sunday he would hike the mile and a half to the Hillsdale County Poorhouse. (He was expelled from the school in May 1866 for taking part in a "student rebellion," along with 21 others. He was reinstated and graduated on time with his class in 1869.)

Carleton was quoted as saying about the local poorhouse, "The conditions there are heart-rending. There are people there whose families ought to take care of them and who don't do it. It makes one sick with pity."

Hillsdale County Medical Care Facility and Rehabilitation Center

In 1954, Bob Evans Farms purchased the Poor Farm property to build a sausage processing plant. They donated the poorhouse to the Hillsdale Historical Society. The historical society restored it as a tribute to Will Carleton and to be used as a local museum.

Hillsdale County Medical Care Facility in 2019

CHAPTER THIRTY-ONE

Houghton County Poor Farm/Infirmary

On the south shore of Portage Lake, in Hancock Township, on the Kewanee Waterway, was the Houghton County Poor Farm (later referred to as the Houghton County Infirmary). It was on the south shore of Portage Lake. Like many poorhouses of the day, it didn't have bathrooms and the only objects for washing and hygiene was tubs. Heat was via wood stoves and residents were given tea twice a day, with three meals per day, served with meats and fresh vegetables.

The insane were sent to the State Asylum in Traverse City. If there were any children, they received six months of schooling in the winter. In the year 1881, there were 38 residents in the Poor Farm. The county also helped care for 150 paupers maintained outside of the Poor Farm, and 10 more county residents in the State Asylum. The total amount paid in 1881 for care of the poor was $13,955.97.

In an 1896 report, it was stated that the heat for the building was provided by the Spence hot water system. For bathing there was a tub and hot and cold running water. It was said that the paupers received "kind but firm" treatment in the report, and the food was described as "plain, substantial, of good quality, and abundant." There was a hospital next to the infirmary that treated the residents. There were no separate accommodations for the idiotic or insane. Children went to a schoolhouse that was located just 200 feet from the infirmary for ten months a year.

In 1920, there were 77 paupers in the Poor Farm; in 1930 the number rose to 93. The farm ultimately closed in 1955.

Houghton County Poor Farm

CHAPTER THIRTY-TWO

Huron County Almshouse

In 1875 the county bought 200 acres for $600, located a mile west of Bad Axe. It was in Colfax Township, and the property was to be used as a Poor Farm. First, ten acres were cleared, and a barn built. The next year the Poorhouse was built, and it was frame and had two stories with an attic. It had 25 rooms, and cost about $4,000. In 1877, after the farm was in operation, a second barn and two sheds were built.

Most reports were good—good food, clothing adequate for each season, with nicely furnished rooms. There were regular checks on the residents by a physician three times-a-week and more if needed. Tubs and pails were used for bathing, and there were two separate rooms (referred to as "cells") for the idiotic and insane. The average number of residents was usually around ten, and the annual cost of the Poor Farm was about $3,500 a year.

In 1910 there were 23 residents including 13 men and 10 women. The 1920 numbers were 25 men and 9 women, with 26 men and 14 women in 1930.

In 1936 the facility was cited for overcrowding, with 87 men and 44 women. In 1938 the numbers were down to 62 men and 24 women.

Huron County Poor Farm

CHAPTER THIRTY-THREE

Ingham County Poor Farm

In 1884 the Superintendents of the Poor purchased a structure for $500, to be used for a poor farm to house the indigent of Ingham County. A farm with 80 acres (35 of them improved) was purchased for $500 and it had been updated with an addition costing $100. The value of the produce raised on the farm in 1848 was judged to be worth $174.25.

According to an 1896 state report, the poorhouse, in Meridian Township, was in good condition, the food was plain and wholesome, the clothing was comfortable, and the treatment of paupers was humane. The facility was heated by two furnaces. When there were children they were sent to the public schools.

Ingham County Home Cemetery a.k.a. the Poor
Farm Cemetery in Okemos, Michigan

In 1910 there were 66 residents, 43 men and 23 women, and in 1920 there were 48 men and 23 women. In 1930, the Great Depression brought 116 men and 46 women, and in 1935 there were 136 men and 40 women. In 1936 Ingham County was commended in a report as having one of the best poor facilities in the state of Michigan. In 1938 there were 108 men and 62 women under the care of the Ingham County Home.

CHAPTER THIRTY-FOUR

Ionia County Home

In 1855 the Ionia County Board voted to start looking for 80 acres of land to use as a Poor Farm. The Superintendents of the Poor were instructed to bring a list of buildings that would be needed for a poor farm to the next meeting. Two thousand dollars was delegated to be used. Up until 1856 Ionia County didn't have a place for the poor to go—the poor received assistance from the township where they lived. This rarely exceeded $400 for the whole county per year.

The Younger farm was purchased in Ronald Township for $1,644.33 and the buildings made habitable. In the winter of 1856 paupers moved in. The poor house would be given $1500 to $2,000 for maintenance per year. But the original place was deemed inadequate and in 1870 plans were made for the erection of a new Poor Farm.

Ora Waterbury was given $9,791.57 to build the new, brick county home. Once completed, including the steam heat, the total cost ran to $10,722.07. In 1875, another $1,000 was appropriated to complete the interior of the second story.

In 1896 a state report gave the facility good grades and said it was kept in good repair. Tubs and pails were used for bathing. Heat was from a furnace and stoves, the paupers received "kind treatment," and good discipline was said to be maintained.

The report said the food was "wholesome and substantial" and the clothing was distributed according to the season and needs of the residents. A physician was "on call" and visited the facility upon request of the Keeper. Accommodations for the insane were limited, and it was reported by the administrators that they "get along with the idiotic as best they can." Children were found new homes or sent to the State Public School.

The Poor Farm suffered a fire in 1907, destroying the structure. The residents were farmed out while a new, $37,000 facility was built on a different site, closer to Ionia, in Berlin Township on West Riverside Drive.

In 1910 there were 43 residents of the Ionia County Home, 30 men and 15 women. For 1920, the count grew to 48 men and 30 women. With the Depression dawning in 1930, there were 89 men and 39 women living at the County Home. In 1938 there were 108 men and 25 women.

In 1936 the Poor Farm was given good grades by the Michigan Welfare Department. Later the name was changed to the Ionia Reformatory and it became a State Hospital. During Michigan's eugenics phase in the 1930s and 1940s, it was one of the places where they would sterilize the people not deemed of "good reproductive stock".

According to reports, the Berlin Township facility went from "magnificent" to "a state of neglect" over the next 50 years. Circa 1957 the farm closed and was torn down. The residents were given other forms of care. The property is now part of Ionia State Park.

There is a small poor farm cemetery in Ronald Township, the site of the first Poor Farm, with 45 burials. At the site of the Berlin Township County Home, there is a cemetery with 55 burials. This is known as the Ionia County Infirmary Burial Place and is on W. Riverside between Ionia and Saranac.

Ionia County Home/Reformatory

Ionia County Reformatory

CHAPTER THIRTY-FIVE

Iosco County Poor Farm

The Iosco County Board ruled that "The need for relief was caused by several common conditions, such as sickness or death of the husband or wife, or the inability of some injured and elderly to work and support themselves and their families." Stipends were given to those able to stay at home, and others went to the Poor Farm.

In 1871 Iosco County bought 320 acres to be used for a Poor Farm. The land was located on Spartan Road, between Plank and Kobs Road, in Section 10 in Tawas Township. The first house used burned down in October 1871 and so a log house on the property was renovated.

A Keeper of the Poor was paid $500 a year to manage the Poor Farm, including providing "good wholesome food." The farm had a lot of pine timber, which they sold to a contractor in 1874. The Keeper of the Poor maintained a Journal, in which he recorded:

a. the inmate's name

b. age, sex, residence

c. date admitted, cause of pauperism

d. date discharged, cause of discharge, and notations if blind, mute, epileptic, idiotic, or insane

Some of the Poor Farm's children were adopted through the courts and some were sent to the State School in Coldwater. If judged insane, the patient would be sent to one of the State Hospitals at Pontiac, Traverse City, or Kalamazoo.

A Poor Farm Cemetery was located along Spartan Road. The unmarked, un-fenced cemetery is still owned by the county, even though the rest of the Poor Farm property has been sold.

In 1889 the County Supervisors objected to the $4,000 annual cost of the Poor Farm and facetiously said that it would be cheaper to put them up in a Mt. Clemens bathhouse/hotel.

An 1896 report said that the treatment of paupers was good. A furnace was used for heat, and there was a special brick building in the back of the property to house the idiotic and insane. There was a district school one mile from the Poor Farm.

The county would give money for people to take the train or bus to relatives or friends who would care for them. Some were sent out of the county, state, or country.

In 1910 the Poor Farm population was eleven, nine men and two women. In 1920 there were 11 men and one woman and in 1930 it was six men and one woman. In 1938 the Poor Farm had 8 men and 10 women—it didn't happen too often where there were more women than men in a county's poor farm population.

In 1921 the Poor Farm was moved to a 120-acre site in Tawas Township. Unfortunately, in a 1936 report, the farm was unfavorably described as "filthy."

When Social Security benefits and other social safety nets became available in the county, the Poor Farm was phased out.

*Two barns are all that remained of the Iosco Poor Farm
at the time of this picture by Michael Burns.*

CHAPTER THIRTY-SIX

Iron County Poor House/Infirmary

In 1896 the State of Michigan reported on the Iron County Poorhouse, located in the township of Crystal Falls, about two and a half miles from the Village of Crystal Falls. The inspection found the facility "first-class." Bathing facilities included a big tub and hot and cold running water. Wood stoves with good ventilation warmed the house. It was said the treatment of paupers was good, and that "order is kept with firmness, but kindness." Food was abundant, most of it grown on the farm, and clothing was "plentiful and good."

Accommodations for the idiotic and insane were not needed, and there were no children on the farm in 1896.

The next Iron County Poor House was built in 1901 on US-2 Highway near Crystal Falls. In 1910 the Iron County Hospital in Crystal Falls had six residents, all of them men. In 1920 the population had grown to 11 men and one woman. In 1925 there were 12 men and one woman, and in the Depression year of 1930 the population was 52 men and 17 women. By 1935 the population had risen to 236 men and 228 women as mining jobs dwindled. The number of men in 1938 was 176 with 80 women.

In 1930 Iron County opened a new, $80,000 Poor House in Iron City for its 69 paupers. The building had two stories and a basement and was modern by 1930 standards, including refrigeration, a telephone system, an elevator, a forced-air heating and ventilation system, and a medical facility.

In 1938, during the Great Depression, the Infirmary offered meals to the public for 9 cents a person.

Poorhouse resident in Iron River, Michigan, in the Iron County Poor House

CHAPTER THIRTY-SEVEN

Isabella County Poor Farm

Isabella County Poor Farm, then and now

In 1860 the Isabella County Board of Supervisors appointed Superintendents of the Poor and voted to set aside $190 for support of the poor. This method of caring for the poor, by giving them money, continued until 1864, when it was determined that a county Poor Farm was needed. It was voted to spend $3,000 to purchase 160 acres of land and build a County Poor Farm, which they did. The land was bought from William F. Payne. It was in Chippewa Township, about seven miles from the county seat, Mt. Pleasant.

In 1886, in the Committee on the Poor's report, they deplored the indigent condition of the Indians in the area, stating that many were very old and blind. More aid was pledged. Also documented was the institution's income from the sale of farm products.

An 1896 report stated that the males stayed in the main building and that it was in good shape. The females dwelled in the same building as the Keeper, a building it was said should be enlarged. The men also had good bathing facilities including a tub with water from a cistern, while the women only had pails and small tubs.

There was no harsh treatment of the inmates, and clothing was comfortable. Heat was by wood stove; the wood being provided by the farm. The food was substantial, healthful and well-cooked. The report concluded with compliments about the good medical care. The insane and idiotic were "treated the same as everyone else," but there was a special cell if anyone became unruly.

In 1910 the Isabella County Farm in Mt. Pleasant had 25 residents, 17 men and 8 women. By 1911 the farm was well-run, with nourishing food and adequate medical care for the farm's charges. The farm itself appreciated in value to be worth $20,000 in 1911. For 1911, $9,000 was appropriated for the care of 26 residents.

In 1920 there were 25 men and 12 women; in 1925 it was 31 men and 10 women.

In 1930 the Isabella County Farm received an unfavorable state report in which it was stated that the farm was overcrowded, with 39 men and 12 women. It was reported that there were 16 men sleeping in the basement. In 1938 there were 43 men and seven women, so it didn't get much better.

CHAPTER THIRTY-EIGHT

Jackson County Poor Farm/Infirmary

The Jackson County Poorhouse/Poor Farm/Infirmary was built in 1838 on 180 acres, northwest of the City of Jackson, Section 19 of Blackman Township, on the aptly named County Farm Road. The cross street is Dearing Road. Seventy acres of the farm were improved. It was near what are now the Seventh Day Adventist School, and the Seventh Day Adventist Community Service Building.

In 1886 there was a fire at the poorhouse facility, killing five, three men and two women. The other 35 residents escaped without harm. The deceased residents were identified as "Dolly Martin, aged sixty years, insane, an inmate for twelve years; Kate Avery, seventy, insane, inmate for ten years; Jane Atkins, seventy, insane, an inmate ten years; Zina Boynton, ninety-two, deaf, and Charles Elliott, seventy-two, blind." This was as written in the Decatur County Journal.

The Jackson County Poor Farm/Infirmary

The Jackson County Infirmary

The 1886 fire burned the $12,000 building which had just been built a few years prior. The fire started in the resident's kitchen, although the specifics weren't known. The whole interior was destroyed, even burning up the resident's clothes, forcing them to run naked into the January weather, when the temperature was ten degrees below zero.

An 1896 report describes the facility as in good condition, with bathrooms on both floors of the two-story facility, as well as bathing accommodations. Heat was by steam and open fireplaces. There were insane wards in both the male and female departments, food and clothing needs were well-met, and a school was located one-half mile from the facility.

One of the residents of the house was William Mills, the first man to issue the Sanders' spelling book, and was worth at one time a quarter of a million dollars.

Only foundations remain where the Poorhouse was. There is a fenced area near the road that is the Poor Farm Cemetery. There are some records of the people buried there, although there are little in the way of headstones.

In 1910 it was called the Jackson County Infirmary. The Poor Farm residents were later moved to the Jackson County Medical Care Facility on Lansing Ave.

The original Poor Farm structure had been vacant for a few years in the late 1950s when a few men escaped from Jackson State Prison and hid out in it for a few days. In the early 1960s the building was torn down.

CHAPTER THIRTY-NINE

Kalamazoo County Poor Farm

Kalamazoo County Poor Farm

Before establishing a poor farm in 1838, Kalamazoo County appropriated fifty dollars to help the county's poor and in 1840 increased the amount to eight-hundred dollars. From 1839 to 1842, $1,067.56 was spent on the poor. The county rented places to house the indigent until 1842, when It was decided that the county should purchase a farm to be used to accommodate them. Even though it was a farm it was called the County Home and officially opened in 1844.

Some of the reasons for admission to the Poor Farm included alcoholism, unwed pregnancy, blindness or hearing impairment, being an orphan, old age, or even working as a prostitute. Parents who were unable to support a child would take the child to the Poor Farm.

The Kalamazoo County Farm's buildings were originally built as a Utopian community dedicated to Fourierist principles and not related to the county.. Calling it "Associationism," they followed a set of political, economic, and social ideas formulated by French intellectual Charles Fourier (1772–1837).

These included communal ideas of proponents living and working together and were often referred to as "Utopian Socialism." The group was called the "Alphadelphian Society." In 1844 the group bought 3,000 acres in Comstock Township, near Gladstone, in Kalamazoo County, and built a large mansion. For four years they worked at building an ideal society where everyone worked for the common good. At one time the group had over 300 members, but the group dwindled, and finally disbanded in 1848.

The County of Kalamazoo purchased the Comstock Township (later Galesburg) property from the Associates and turned it into the Kalamazoo County Farm, to house the mentally impaired and indigent. This was the second property the county had bought; they had previously purchased a 111-acre plot but sold it. The new one they settled on in 1849 contained 173 acres and contained the buildings the left from when the Alphadelphians lived there.

The main building the Alphadelphians built was a large wood, 2-story, L-shaped structure. A barn was added to the property in 1872 for $700. Previous buildings on the property, including a horse barn and a granary, were given improved foundations. For $150 each, a new corn-house and hog-house were built.

Most notably, in the 1870s, a separate infirmary building was built for the injured and the sick for $250. A new washhouse was built for $100. A new furnace was added for $250 and $1,000 was spent on roofs and other improvements. An apple orchard was planted and over a mile of fence was added to the property.

The "incurably insane," while housed in a separate building in the early 1840s, were sent to the State House by the 1850s. Children were sent to be schooled at the State Public School in Coldwater.

In 1848 the value of the produce raised on the farm totaled $548. In 1854 there were 31 paupers at the County Farm—16 adults and 15 children. Five of the adults were insane. In 1910 there were 52 paupers, 48 men and 4 women.

The 1876 Michigan report on its poorhouses called the general condition of the Kalamazoo Poor Farm "first-class." Complimented in the report were its hot and cold running water, bathtubs, steam heat radiators, meals, treatment of residents, and ventilation.

In 1910 the Kalamazoo County Poor Farm in Galesburg had 52 residents, 48 men and 4 women. The facility was later referred to as the Kalamazoo County Rest Home.

In 1919 four residents died after eating food contaminated with roach poison. In 1920 the facility housed 72 men and 19 women. By 1925 it was 91 men and 22 women and in 1930 it was 153 men and 37 women. In 1935 it was 156 men and 56 women and in 1938 there were 101 men and 59 women.

It was business as usual until 1936, when the facility was cited for overcrowding with 165 men and 55 women. In the report, it was stated that men were sleeping in the basement of the infirmary and that there was only one toilet for 25 women to use. The facility closed in the early 1970s. Today, the land that was once the Poor Farm is part of River Oaks Park on M-96 between Comstock and Galesburg.

The Michigan Asylum for the Insane opened in 1859 on Oakland Drive (originally known as Asylum Avenue) in Kalamazoo. It was the first facility for the insane in Michigan and was named the Kalamazoo State Hospital in 1911, the Kalamazoo Regional Psychiatric Hospital in 1978, and then in 1995 was renamed the Kalamazoo Psychiatric Hospital, the name it's known by today.

Kalamazoo State Hospital

All of the original buildings have been replaced by more modern counterparts, except for the historic water tower. The water tower was built in 1895, is 175 feet tall, and was added to the National Register of Historic Places in 1973. It has three water storage tanks within it.

Kalamazoo Hospital Water Tower

CHAPTER FORTY

Kalkaska County Infirmary

Kalkaska County was formed in 1840 in the northern portion of Michigan's Lower Peninsula. It was called Wabassee County until 1843 and has over 80 lakes. Most of the county is in the Pere Marquette State Forest.

The Kalkaska County Infirmary in Mancelona had 13 patients in 1910, 10 men and 3 women. In 1920 there were nine men and four women, and in 1925 it was ten men and three women. For the Depression year of 1930 there were 16 men and five women, and in 1935 there were 35 men and two women.

In 1936 they were closed due to a report that the infirmary was "unfit for human habitation." At the end of the year the population was 22 men and two women. In 1938 they were still in business with 12 men and no women.

CHAPTER FORTY-ONE

Kent County Poor Farm/ County Home

The Kent County Board of Supervisors informed the State of Michigan in 1849 that Kent County was not getting a Poor Farm. They had decided it was much easier to give paupers a stipend for their care than to maintain a poor farm.

Circumstances had changed by 1855 and Kent County purchased 80 acres of land in Section 16 of Paris Township for $1,800. It was southwest of Grand Rapids, on 32nd Street between Breton and Kalamazoo Streets. The paupers moved there in December 1855.

In 1876 a report stated that the buildings were in very good condition and now included 146 acres, most of them improved. Lauded were the seven bathrooms located throughout the building, and the steam heat that the building had good ventilation for.

The report stated that the inmates were treated as kindly as circumstances would permit, and that the rules of the house were strictly enforced. Food, clothing, and health care for the residents was reportedly good. The insane were sent to the Kalamazoo Asylum and children were found homes so no educational arrangements were made.

A new building was built in 1892 and by 1896 there were 238 residents, including men, women, and children. The grounds of the poor farm also included the County Home Cemetery, now known as Maple Grove Cemetery.

The Poor Farm continued into the 1900s and in 1920, with 196 men and 77 women, was called the Kent County Infirmary. In 1925 there were 260 men and 68 women and in 1930 it was 405 men and 64 women. In 1936, with 344 men and 76 women, for a grand total of 420, the facility was cited by the state for good performance.

In the 1950s the facility was renamed the Maple Grove Medical Facility and specialized in chronic illnesses. In 1968 the name was again revised to be the Kent Community Hospital and was moved to the City of Grand Rapids on Fuller Street. The previous site was sold to the Lutheran Church of America and today Luther Village is on the old Poor Farm site. The Maple Grove Medical Facility building was demolished in 1971.

The County Home Cemetery of Kent County was renamed Maple Grove Cemetery.

CHAPTER FORTY-TWO

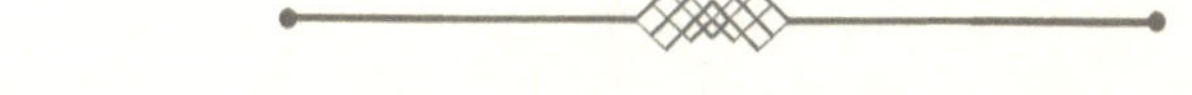

Keweenaw County Poorhouse

Keweenaw County was organized in 1861 and is Michigan's northernmost county, located in the Keweenaw Peninsula. Logging was its first big industry.

In 1870 the Poorhouse had 11 paupers residing there in Grant Township, in this sparsely populated county. In 1876 a state inspection reported that the house was in the Village of Eagle River, on the upper tip of the U.P. in Houghton Township. The report further stated that the building was frame and in good repair but was not owned by the county.

The house had no regular facilities for bathing and heat was by stoves. The resident's clothing was said to be suitable for the climate and the food plain and substantial. When anyone got sick a physician was called, and children attended the public schools. There were no insane or idiotic housed there.

The Keweenaw Poorhouse did not submit census reports to the state from its inception through 1938.

The Keweenaw County-Poorhouse is to the right.

CHAPTER FORTY-THREE

Lake County Poor Farm/Infirmary

In 1885 the Village of Baldwin, which was the County Seat of Lake County, voted to provide $2,500 for the building of a poor farm. It was built and an 1896 inspection report stated that the house and farm buildings were in good condition and that the bathing facilities had hot and cold water with pails and bath tubs. Heat was from stoves.

The report further stated that treatment of the paupers and kind and humane and that corporeal punishment was not allowed. The food was good and fresh, the clothing properly seasonable. The medical care was good and the insane had a separate room. Children attended the "common school" while at the home.

In 1910 the population of the farm was seven: six men and one woman. In 1920 there were nine men and two women inhabitants of the farm. In 1925 there were eight men and no women. In 1930 there were nine men and eight women and in 1938 there were nine men and one woman. The facility operated from 1885 until 1954, usually with 12 to 15 residents.

When a resident died, if the body wasn't claimed, they were buried in the potter's field section of the Chase Township Cemetery, just down the road from the farm. The house still stands as of 2019 at Hawkins Road, south of Highway U. S. 10 in Chase Township.

The area was near the Pere Marquette Railroad and was called Poor Farm Corner.

Other structures on the property included an infirmary behind the main building, other outbuildings, and a large red barn which burned down in the 1970s.

Lake County Poor Farm Barn

The old Lake County Poor Farm can be seen in the distance in this Google Earth shot.

CHAPTER FORTY-FOUR

Lapeer County Poor Farm/ Oakdale Eugenics Center

Lapeer County Poor Farm

Lapeer State Home and Training School, Lapeer, Mich.

Lapeer County's Oakdale Center for Developmental Disabilities

In 1896 a state report noted that the Lapeer Farm was in Mayfield Township and was heated by hot water heating and transom ventilation. There was at that time no separate facility for "idiots" or the insane. Food and clothing were good, and children attended the district school. The brick building was two-stories tall with a nine-foot basement, was heated by hot water, had bathtubs with hot and cold water, and a good sewer system. The only complaint in the report was that the inmates' bedrooms were on the second story and had difficulty going downstairs and getting exercise.

In 1897 the Michigan Legislation attempted to pass a Eugenics law but was unsuccessful. The Eugenics Movement had just begun. Eugenics was defined as "a set of beliefs and practices aimed at improving the genetic quality of the human population by excluding genetic groups judged to be inferior and promoting those deemed superior."

The Michigan Legislature had better luck in 1913 when they passed a law, *Public Act 34: 1913*, "an act to authorize the sterilization of mentally defective persons." The law allowed forced sterilization of the "mentally defective or insane." However, only one sterilization was performed before the practice was stopped by the Michigan Supreme Court with the court case, the "Haynes vs. Lapeer Circuit Judge."

In 1923 a new sterilization law was passed, and as amended in 1925 stood up under scrutiny in several court cases in 1925 and 1926. The way sterilization would occur included vasectomy, salpingectomy (surgical removal of a fallopian tube), and x-rays. In 1929 castration was added to the list, and by 1938, twenty had been performed—all on sex offenders.

By 1929 the people the law expanded to include idiots, imbeciles, the feebleminded, the insane, epileptics, sexual perverts, and moral degenerates. The law included people in state institutions, including the Poor Farms, and the public at large. Even later the list included "frequent masturbation" and being an only child of a mother having had frequent miscarriages as grounds for sterilization. The ultimate goal was to weed out the "unfit" and create a race of "strong and fit men and women."

Circa 1913 in North Carolina, in the Smith vs. the Board of Examiners case, it was determined that:

"The Michigan statute is not perfect. Undoubtedly time and experience will bring changes in many of its workable features. But it is expressive of a state policy apparently based on the growing belief that, due to the alarming increase in the number of degenerates, criminals, feeble-minded, and insane, our race is

facing the greatest peril of all time. Whether this belief is well founded is not for this court to say. Unless for the soundest constitutional reasons, it is our duty to sustain the policy which the state has adopted. As we before have said, it is no valid objection that it imposes reasonable restraints upon natural and constitutional rights. It is an historic fact that every forward step in the progress of the race is marked by an interference with individual liberties."

Further, it was stated:

"It is known by conservative estimate that there are at least 20,000 recognized feeble-minded persons in the State of Michigan—eight times as many as can be segregated in State institutions. The Michigan Home and Training School at Lapeer is full to overflowing with these unfortunates, and hundreds of others are on the waiting lists. That they are a serious menace to society no one will question.

In view of these facts, what are the legal rights of this class of citizens as to the procreation of children? It is true that the right to beget children is a natural and constitutional right, but it is equally true that no citizen has any rights superior to the common welfare. Acting for the public good, the state, in the exercise of its police powers, may always impose reasonable restrictions upon the natural and constitutional rights of its citizens. Measured by its injurious effect upon society, what right has any citizen or class of citizens to beget children with an inherited tendency to crime, feeble-mindedness, idiocy or imbecility?"

Lapeer County established the Michigan Home for the Feebleminded and Epileptic in 1893. It was a "State Home" as well as a County Farm. It went by many names, including the Michigan Home and Training School, the Lapeer State Home and Training School, the Oakdale Center for Developmental Disabilities, and the Lapeer Poor Farm.

According to records, 2,337 people were sterilized in the Lapeer County Home. Other institutions, including the Ionia Reformatory,

Jackson State Prison, the University of Michigan hospital, and other county and state facilities, performed sterilizations. However, no institution had anywhere near the number of sterilizations as Lapeer's County Home.

One of the main proponents of the Eugenics Theory was Battle Creek, Michigan's John Harvey Kellogg, creator of Corn Flakes and founder of the Kellogg Sanitarium. (Other proponents were Alexander Graham Bell and Planned Parenthood founder Margaret Sanger.) In 1914 Kellogg conducted the first meeting of the Race Betterment Conference. The purpose of the five-day event was to "study the cause of and cure for race degeneracy." Eugenics was thought to be a cure for "alcoholism, poverty, criminality, sexual promiscuity, and 'feeblemindedness.'"

PROCEEDINGS

OF THE

First National Conference on Race Betterment

January 8, 9, 10, 11, 12, 1914

BATTLE CREEK, MICHIGAN

PUBLISHED BY THE RACE BETTERMENT FOUNDATION

EDITED BY THE SECRETARY

"To be a good animal is the first requisite to success in life, and to be a Nation of good animals is the first condition of national prosperity."
—Herbert Spencer.

A Group of Physicians and Other Specialists Who Gave Their Services in Examining and Scoring Participants in the Fitter Families Contest

Before Eugenics was scientifically discredited, 3,786 people were subjected to forced sterilization, 74% of them women. Sterilizations were at their peak in the 1930s and 1940s and didn't end until the 1970s. Most of the buildings of "The Facility" or the "State Home," as it was last referred to, were closed in 1992 and demolished in 1996. The land was sold to Mott Community College.

Lapeer County Home in 1951

Originally known as "The County Poor Farm," in the 1950s it became known as "The Infirmary." As the 1960s brought Medicare and Medicaid to the forefront and nursing centers became skilled nursing centers, the facility became known as "The Lapeer County Extended Care Facility" and "Suncrest," because it is located on Suncrest Drive. In 1971 it became the Lapeer County Medical Care Facility. Today it has over 200 beds and treats dementia as well as specializing in skilled nursing.

1930s Aerial View of the Lapeer complex

Michigan House for the Feeble Minded

Lapeer County Complex in 1948

Lapeer County Home and Complex

Lapeer State Home and Training School

Lapeer Co. Poor Farm Cemetery gravestone

CHAPTER FORTY-FIVE

Leelanau County Poor Farm

Leelanau County was set off in 1840, but not organized until 1863. It is known for its wineries and as the home of Sleeping Bear Dunes, noted in a 2011 survey as "the most beautiful place in America."

The Leelanau County Poor Farm in Maple City had 19 residents in 1910, 13 men and 6 women. In 1920, there were 5 men and 7 women and in 1925 there were 8 men and 3 women. In the Great Depression year of 1931, the Poor Farm population went up to 10 men and 3 women.

In 1938 there were 15 men and 9 women. Clearly, there weren't a lot of paupers making their way through Leelanau County as even the Depression didn't raise the Poor Farm numbers much.

Leelanau County Poor Farm Barn

The same Poor Farm Barn as it looks after restoration.

CHAPTER FORTY-SIX

Lenawee County Infirmary

The Lenawee Poor Farm in Madison Township was purchased in 1835 for $1,500 and had 80 acres, 50 of which were improved. A house was built in 1836 cost $500. Another house was built in 1846 for $180 and outhouses were built for $100. The farm made $148 from its produce in 1848.

According to an 1876 inspection, the buildings were in good shape and the farm had a new hog house, hen house, tool house, and barn. It was a two-story brick house with a high attic. This made it practically a three-story building. Separate men's and women's dormitories were maintained, bathing facilities were good, with hot and cold water, and there was good food for the inmates.

The report concluded with saying that "the house is quite old, poorly planned, but is kept clean and orderly."

In 1910 the Lenawee County Infirmary in Adrian had 60 patients, 33 men and 27 women. In 1920 there were 48 men and 30 women and in 1925, 68 men and 52 women lived there. In 1930 there were 91 men and 43 women.

The Lenawee County Infirmary was said to be well-maintained in a 1936 report by the Michigan Welfare Department. The year of the report the Infirmary housed 88 men and 25 women. In 1938 there were 72 men and 29 women.

CHAPTER FORTY-SEVEN

Livingston County Infirmary

An 1896 report stated that the infirmary was six miles from Howell, in a two-story brick house, with the sexes separated. Bathrooms with tubs were provided and there was a good supply of water, good drainage, and good ventilation. There was steam heat.

A second building served as a hospital and a home for the sick, infirm, and elderly. Tubs and lavatories were available, but fire escapes were needed. The commissioner said, "The house (is) in excellent condition and the inmates well cared for and contented."

The Livingston County Infirmary in Howell had 22 indigent residents in 1910, 19 of which were men and three were women. In 1920 there were 19 men and five women, and in 1925 there were 19 men and seven women. The year of 1930 was the dawn of the Depression and there were 23 men and six women; in 1935 there were 31 men and six women and in 1938 there were 33 men and 12 women.

CHAPTER FORTY-EIGHT

Luce County Poor Farm

In 1876 it was reported that the Poor Farm main building was a small, story and a half, frame building. It was reported as having no conveniences and being too small, but an addition was being built.

In 1910, Luce County Poor Farm of Newberry had 8 residents, 6 men and 2 women. The average number was between six and seven residents. In 1911 the Board of Supervisors started looking for and found a new farm location. This was because the old one had only five acres and couldn't produce enough food to feed the residents.

In 1920 the Poor Farm had 34 male residents and six females. In 1925 there were 15 men and one woman. In 1930 there were 40 men and no women; in 1935 there were 35 men and still no women, and in 1938 there was 19 men and one woman housed at the Poor Farm.

In 1934 the Keeper of the Poor was arrested for assault after he hit the Superintendent of the Poor upon being told he was being let go. This was following an argument over a truck belonging to the facility.

CHAPTER FORTY-NINE

Mackinac County Poorhouse/Farm

Mackinac County was established in 1818 as Michilimackinac County and was originally a French trading post. It was one of the first counties of Michigan and the county seat is St. Ignace. Calling itself the Gateway to the Upper Peninsula, it is located right off the Mackinac Bridge.

In an 1890 report, the Mackinac County Poor Farm was documented as being in the township of Brevort in the village of Allenville. This was about ten miles from St. Ignace.

The main building was a wooden, two-story building in fair condition. Bathing accommodations was with bath tubs. The building's heat came from stoves and heating drums. Ventilation was from windows and doors.

The report said that the paupers were well-treated and given good, wholesome food and warm, adequate clothing. When sick they were well-provided with physicians and nursing. There were no "idiotic" or insane people in the house, so no separate accommodations were needed.

The farm had 80 acres, 30 of which were under cultivation. At the time of the report there was just one inmate in the house. The house averaged two inmates per year in the early 1900s.

State reports give the 1920 population of the Poorhouse as 19 men and three women and in 1925 it was 44 men and eight women. In 1930 there were 42 men and 10 women, while in 1938 there were 19 men and no women living in the Poorhouse.

CHAPTER FIFTY

Macomb County Poor Farm

In 1837 the Board of Supervisors of Macomb County authorized the purchase of 40 acres for use as a poor farm. The Superintendents of the Poor purchased an additional 94 acres. When the Poor Farm opened in Mt. Clemens in 1840, 60 of the acres had been improved. It eventually grew to 240 improved acres.

In 1867, the oven at the Poor Farm caught on fire, burning the whole house down. It was voted to provide a new Poor House funded by $10,000 in taxes. The new structure built in 1868 was made of brick and could house 120 residents. Circa 1900 electricity was added to the Poor House, and an elevator was added. In 1901 there were two brick buildings at the Poor Farm site—they were two-story brick structures with a basement, one for the men and one for the women. Both buildings were steam-heated with "fair" sewerage and ventilation.

In 1883 the poor were classified into groups—the clean and rational occupied one building, and the "filthy" were sent to another building. Inmates took care of the idiotic in another area, while the insane were housed in another facility with a high fence surrounding it.

Women had a wash house and wash tub at their disposal; men were told to bathe in the Clinton River. The able-bodied residents were expected to work on the farm. Clothing was made by the women residents.

An 1896 report describes the poorhouse as a two-story brick building with a basement. It was remarked that sometimes paupers were housed in the basement. Bathtubs were provided. The report remarked, "House very clean though old, and without many of the modern improvements."

In 1910 the Poor Farm had 36 residents, 27 men and nine women. An addition was added in 1923, expanding the facility to nearly 20,000 square feet, three times its original size. It was used as a medical building. Indoor plumbing was added, and it became known as the "County Infirmary." The insane were sent to the St. Joseph Sanitarium, which was later renamed St. Joseph Hospital.

In 1920 there were 42 men and 12 women on the Poor Farm and in 1925 there were 36 men and 20 women. In 1930 there were 57 men and 15 women; in 1935 there were 148 men and 34 women, and in 1938, 138 men and 62 women were housed at the Macomb County Poor Farm.

Dr. H.G. Berry left several thousand dollars to the county to establish the Martha T. Berry Hospital for the indigent, to be named for his wife. In 1950 the indigent residents were transferred there. The original building was renovated for $100,000 and the Welfare Department was housed on the bottom floor, while the Macomb County Library was on the second floor.

Besides the medical building, other buildings on the premises included a wood shed, a hen house, piggery, butcher shop, barn, corn crib, tool shed, ice house, laundry house, a carriage house, an underground coal bin, a milk house, and a canning house. Another building was the "Pest House," used to quarantine people with infectious diseases such as tuberculosis or smallpox.

The last farming took place in 1963. When the library and Welfare Department moved to new structures, the main poorhouse building was vacant for many years. The Macomb County Jail, located in the same area, planned an expansion and wanted to expand their parking also. It was decided to raze the old poorhouse to make room for additional parking.

Leading the effort to preserve the building in 1998 was Macomb County Historian Cynthia Donahue. But asbestos problems and other code violations doomed the structure and the main building was demolished in 2001. A memorial was dedicated in 2004 by the Macomb County Historical Commission.

St. Joseph Sanitarium in Mt. Clemens, Macomb County; later St. Joseph's Hospital

Macomb County Poor Farm in Mt. Clemens, Michigan

Martha T. Berry Medical Facility

Macomb County Poorhouse

CHAPTER FIFTY-ONE

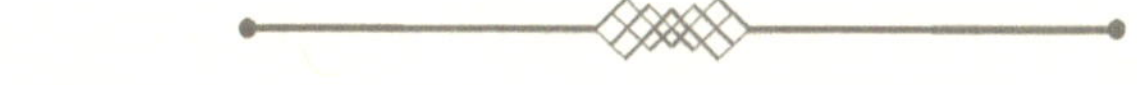

Manistee County Poorhouse

An 1876 report states that the poorhouse, located about four miles from the City of Manistee, was a two-story brick building, had a high basement, and was in "first-class" condition. Men and women slept in separate quarters and the facility had good food, hot and cold water, good bathing facilities, sewerage and ventilation, and fire escapes! It was heated by three furnaces and had "ample hospital wards." The dining room was judged a little too small.

Although usually referred to in state records as the Manistee County Poorhouse, it was located on a farm, with the produce used to feed the residents.

The report said that the treatment of paupers was "fair and humane." The food was of good quality, "well-cooked and well-served and plentiful." There was a whole floor that was used as a hospital ward. There was a separate room for insane males and another separate room for insane females that were used until the patient could be transferred to an insane asylum.

The Keeper and his mate got along well with the idiotic and feeble-minded, so no special provisions were made for them. A district school was less than half a mile from the institute, and the children were later transferred to the State Public School.

In 1903, lightning struck 7 out of 8 farm buildings at the Poor Farm. A local newspaper, the *L'Anse Sentinel,* described it thusly:

"Seven large frame buildings at Manistee, belonging to the Manistee county poor farm, were destroyed by fire Saturday evening. The buildings were struck by lightning. Only the brick poorhouse stands. The loss will approximate $8,000."

In 1910 the Manistee County Poorhouse had 51 residents, 37 men and 14 women. This number hadn't changed much by 1920, when the numbers were 38 men and 13 women. In the Depression year of 1930 the numbers went down to 29 men and no women. In 1938 the number was 12 men and no women.

CHAPTER FIFTY-TWO

Marquette County Poor Farm and Poor House

The Poor Farm and Poor House were in the south part of Marquette City. In 1881 a report stated that the pauper's labor was valued at $300 for the year and the profit from the farm produce was $500. The report went on to state, "amount paid for official services to the poor, and for their transportation and support, $1,939.91; medicine, funerals, food, fuel, clothing and other expenses in aid of extern poor, $15,867.17; average cost of each intern pauper for the year, $57.88. The total amount expended during the year in the care and support of the poor was $23,912.44."

There were two births in the poorhouse during the year, one legitimate and one illegitimate. There was one death and the number of people who received county aid not housed in the Poorhouse was 1,043 poor, one insane person, and one deaf and dumb person. The total number of people helped throughout 1883 was 1, 154.

An 1896 State of Michigan inspection reveals that the Marquette Poor Farm had a bath tub, with hot and cold running water. It was heated by steam and had stoves that were used when there was extremely cold weather.

The inspection report mentioned that there were light labor tasks provided for those who wanted to work. Food, clothing, and medical care was good, the insane were sent to an asylum and children to a school just three blocks away from the facility.

The 1910 U.S. Census listed the Marquette County Poor Farm as having 68 residents, 52 men and 16 women. In 1920 there were 60 men and 19 women and in 1930 there were 64 men and 11 women.

CHAPTER FIFTY-THREE

Mason County Poor Farm

Before the Mason County Poor Farm was opened, the county paid $3 a week for indigents to be housed at a Ludington Boarding House.

The Mason County Poor Farm was located southwest of Amber Station in Amber Township. This location was on Dennis Road, between what is now Conrad Road and First Street in present-day Ludington. At first a tract of land was purchased in Victory Township, but the land was discovered to be of "inferior quality" and was sold and the Dennis Road site purchased in 1879.

After the property for the Poor Farm was purchased, a house and barn were quickly built. The house was a frame, two-and-a-half story building that cost $2,800. The barn cost $1,200.

In 1881, forty acres were purchased to go with the original eighty acres, presided over by the County Superintendent of the Poor. The average amount of poor residents in the 1880s was between eight and twelve people.

An 1876 Michigan inspection report reported that the Keeper and his family and the female paupers lived in the main house, and the males were housed in a one-story cottage to the back of the main house. It had good water and sewerage although the bathing facilities were rated as poor. It was heated by wood stoves and it was stated that the house was in good condition but needed new bedding. There was a separate medical building.

In 1910 there were 31 residents, 22 men and 9 women. For 1920 the count was 17 men and six women and in 1925 there were 17 men and six women. In 1930 there were 32 men and six women; in 1935 there were 28 men and six women and in 1938 there were 15 men and five women.

Deceased residents were buried in the Poor Farm Cemetery located on the property.

CHAPTER FIFTY-FOUR

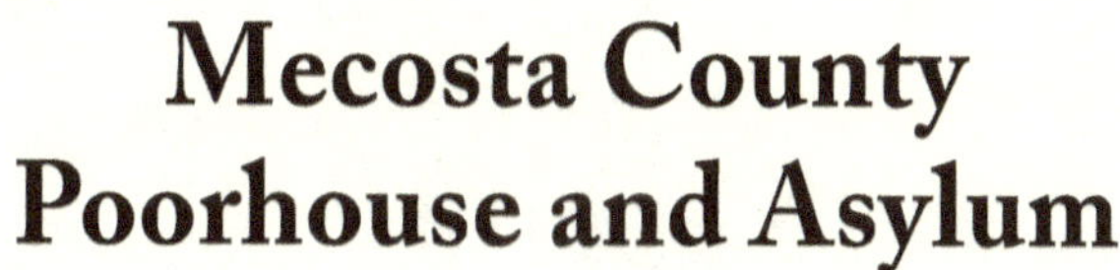

Mecosta County Poorhouse and Asylum

A large poor-house and insane asylum were built a short distance south of the Village of Stanwood in Mecosta County in 1883. However, it burnt down, presumably by arson with incendiaries. Even though a $500 reward was offered, no culprits were found. The seventeen people in the cemetery were re-interred in the town's potter's field.

A new, brick home was built in 1885. A separate building housed the insane. In 1896 a Michigan inspection report describes the new building as a three-story brick building with a high basement and that the top story was not yet used. It further states that the food, clothing and medical care provided the residents was good. The home was heated by furnaces, had good water, sewerage, and bathing facilities, and had enough fire escapes. The sexes were boarded separately.

But the county's bad luck held as in 1899 it too burned, destroying all but one wing and claiming a life. In 1900 another wing was built and in 1910 there were 39 residents, 27 men and 12 women. In 1920 there were 35 men and 13 women; in 1925 there were 60 men and 13 women. In 1930 there were 48 men and 32 women and in 1935 there were 42 men and 12 women.

In 1930 still another wing was built and in 1933 another fire *burned down the whole complex,* this time with three people dying in the blaze!

In 1933 the poorhouse was rebuilt and included a hospital. In 1946 it became the County Convalescent Hospital and in 1951 was newly dedicated as the Mecosta Memorial Hospital.

Mecosta County Poorhouse

CHAPTER FIFTY-FIVE

Menominee Poor House/ County Hospital

When the county was first separated from Delta County in 1861, it was called Bleeker County and then in 1863 was renamed Menominee County after the Native American tribe of the same name. It is in the southern portion of the Upper Peninsula.

An 1896 Michigan report stated that the Poorhouse was located within the city limits of Menominee and was a two-story building with a two-story addition for female paupers. The building was described as having bath rooms and lavatories with good water, and that it was heated with steam although it lacked proper ventilation.

In 1910, the Menominee County Hospital had 24 patients, 18 men and 6 women. In 1920 it had 45 men and six women and in 1925 it had 55 men and 10 women. In 1930 there were 51 men and 5 women. Finally, in 1938 there were 46 men and 15 women.

CHAPTER FIFTY-SIX

Midland County Poor Farm

The Midland County Poor Farm was located about four miles from the city of Midland. It was a story-and-a-half building and heated by stoves. Males and females were boarded separately but all commingled in the yard during the day.

An 1876 Michigan inspection report stated that the main building had portions that were "old and dilapidated," the house was way below average and was a "disgrace to the county."

Midland County Poor Farm

One foible the report documented was that the main building was situated in the lowest part of the property and was prone to flooding. The spring rains would cause a stagnant pond to form in the backyard and the cellar would flood.

The Midland County Poor Farm had 15 residents in the 1910 census—nine men and six women. In 1920 there were 18 men and nine women, and in 1930 there were 22 men and 11 women. In 1938 these numbers grew to 41 men and 12 women.

CHAPTER FIFTY-SEVEN

Missaukee County Poor House

Missaukee County was organized in 1871 after splitting off from Mackinac County. It is in the Traverse City metro area and interestingly, almost 50% of the county belongs to the Christian Reformed Church in North America.

Missaukee County Poor House

The Missaukee County Poor House was located four miles from Lake City, the county seat. An 1896 state report says that it had separate wings for men and women with the Keeper in the middle. The report stated that the house was poorly constructed and had already begun to settle so much that the doors and windows were off-kilter and the walls were cracking. The wings were originally too small and were later enlarged.

The house had no bathrooms but did have running water. It was heated by stoves and furnaces.

In 1910 the Missaukee County Poor House in Lake City had eight residents, seven men and one woman. In 1920 there were 14 men and six women and in 1930 there were 17 men and four women.

CHAPTER FIFTY-EIGHT

Monroe County Poor House

In 1835 the Poorhouse of Monroe County was purchased for $1,000. It was located three and a half miles from Monroe and included 100 acres, fifty of them improved. In 1848 the crops produced were valued at $450.

In 1896 a Michigan inspection report said the facility was "a large two-story brick building, well-planned and a perfect model." The separation of the sexes, water, sewerage, bathing facilities, and ventilation were all lauded as good. A commissioner was quoted as saying, "Everybody happy, everything clean and in good order."

In 1910 this poorhouse in the City of Monroe (formerly Frenchtown) had 33 residents, 26 men and 7 women. In 1920 there were 43 men and 14 women, and in 1930 there were 153 men and 16 women.

One of the most memorable things about the Monroe County Poor House is that they had Clydesdale horses.

Clydesdale horse

CHAPTER FIFTY-NINE

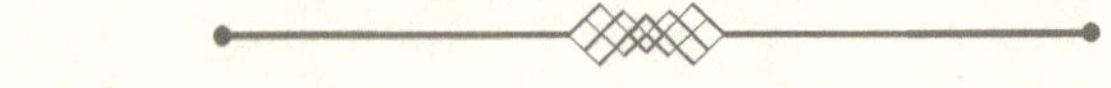

Montcalm County Poor Farm

The four buildings of the Poorhouse for Montcalm County were located six miles from Greenville. A Michigan inspection report from 1896 calls it, "old, out of repair, and inconvenient." The report does say the residents are treated well and with kindness and the house is kept clean despite its age and "inconvenient construction of the buildings." The report ends with stating that many necessary conveniences were lacking, and the county greatly needed a new Poorhouse.

The poor farm was called the Montcalm County Infirmary and there were 38 residents in 1910, 22 men and 16 women. In 1920 there were 28 men and 29 women living in the Infirmary. In 1930 there were 47 men and 14 women.

Montcalm County Poor Farm, courtesy of Judy Hardy

CHAPTER SIXTY

Montmorency County Poorhouse

A Montmorency County resident commented for the "Michigan Dry Manual" that "Four of the six men in our poor house were forced to come here on account of drink."

In 1910, there were seven residents in the Montmorency County Poorhouse, located in Howard. Six were men and one was a woman. In 1920 there were 13 men and three women and in 1925 there were 13 men and four women.

In 1930, there were 12 men and three women in the poorhouse, the same year a state report recommended that the Poorhouse be closed "for economy." There was still some semblance of a poorhouse in 1938 when it was documented that there were four men and two women still in the poorhouse system.

CHAPTER SIXTY-ONE

Muskegon County Poor Farm

The Muskegon County Poor Farm was located about two and a half miles from the county seat, the City of Muskegon, in a "two-story, rambling frame building." In 1896 it had been enlarged and improved in the previous two years. There was separation of the sexes and there were bathing facilities with good water and fair sewerage. It was heated by furnace and lacking a second-story fire escape.

In 1910 the Muskegon County Poor Farm had 51 people, 41 men and 10 women. In 1920 there were 80 men and 45 women living on the farm. In 1930 there were 128 men and 50 women.

Muskegon County Poor Farm

CHAPTER SIXTY-TWO

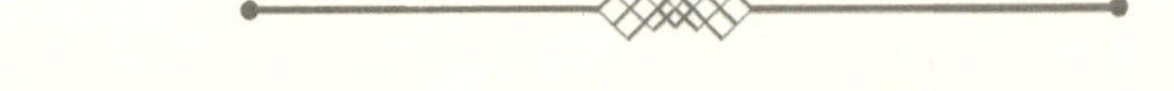

Newaygo County Poor Farm

The Newaygo County Farm was in Fremont, home of Gerber Baby Foods. It was in a two-story frame building, had a good water supply but had poor ventilation and no bathing facilities. In 1918 it was reported that there had been a general overhauling of the poor house which had made the residents more comfortable.

In 1910 the farm had 24 residents, 17 male and seven females. In 1920 there were 24 male inmates and 15 women. In 1930 there were 46 men and 13 women.

Newaygo County Farm

CHAPTER SIXTY-THREE

Oakland County Poor Farm and the Eastern Michigan State Asylum

In 1834 a committee of three was appointed to investigate acquiring property for a facility for the indigent. They decided that they would look for 80 acres, for which $700 was appropriated. The east half of the northeast quarter of Section 2 of Waterford was purchased for $1,050. In 1835 the committee let it be known that the building was ready for occupants.

In 1857 the county made a real-estate exchange, selling the old farm and buying the 350 acres of the Mead Farm, in Section 2 in the northeast and southeast quarters of the township, also in Waterford. The county spent $9.466.40 and received many like-new farm buildings that were already on the land. The Poor Farm residents were moved into the new habitat.

In 1866 the Poor Farm again moved, this time to the northeast corner of Section 2 of the county. With the farm containing 134 acres, in 1866 and 1867 buildings were erected on the new property. An 1867 assessment gave the overall worth of the facility at $32,013. This was broken down to: farm and buildings-$29,295, farming implements-$488, livestock-$1,330, and all other property-$900.

A new main building was erected in 1868, and other buildings on the grounds and part of the facility had farm outbuildings including barns and a hen house. The house contained bathrooms with running water and steam heat.

In 1903 Oakland County decided that the terms "poorhouse" or "almshouse" was not in the best interests of humanitarian thought, and it was decided to henceforth refer to the poorhouse as the County Home.

The usual number of residents cared for usually ranged from 70 to 100, with 2/3 of them being men. In a 1910 U.S. Census Report, it is stated that 74 people are in the Poor Farm, including 53 men and 21 women. By 1910 the farm included a large tool shed, an ice house, a hog house, a corn barn, a large barn, a hen house, and a pumping plant.

In 1920 there were 78 males and 28 females. In 1930 there were 431 males and 326 females. In 1936, when there were 1,381 male inmates and 743 females, the Michigan Welfare Department pronounced the farm "well-run."

Also, in Oakland County, the Eastern Michigan State Asylum for the Insane in Pontiac was founded in 1878 as the third of Michigan's state insane asylums. Due to overcrowding in the Kalamazoo Insane Asylum, in 1873 the Michigan State Legislature appropriated $400,000 to build a new hospital. When it opened at 140 Elizabeth Lake Road in Pontiac five years later, it started with 222 patients. The number increased over the years when it reached a peak in the 1950s with 3,100.

The hospital had the same architect that designed Michigan's State Capitol Building, Elijah E. Myers. He also designed the updates to the hospital in 1882 and 1895. It was further updated in 1906, 1914, and 1938.

In 1911 the facility was renamed the Pontiac State Hospital and in 1973 was renamed the Clinton Valley Center. The number of patients declined until it had about 200 when it closed in 1997. Even though it had been on the Michigan Register of Historical Places since 1983, it was demolished in 2000. A housing subdivision is now on the site.

Pontiac Mental Hospital

Pontiac Mental Asylum in 1876

CHAPTER SIXTY-FOUR

Oceana County Poor House

The Poor House of Oceana County was located about a mile and a half from Hart, the county seat. It was a two-story frame building with bath rooms and fire escapes. It was heated by stoves and male and females had separate sleeping quarters. An 1896 state inspection reported that "the house is much improved (since the previous inspection) a furnace and a cell for the insane (are) needed."

In 1910 the County Poor House had 13 residents, 12 men and one woman. In 1920 there were 24 men and 13 women and in 1930 there were 46 men and 13 women.

Oceana County Poor House in Hart, Michigan

CHAPTER SIXTY-FIVE

Ogemaw County Poor Farm

The Poor Farm of Ogemaw County was a mile and a half from West Branch, the county seat, and was a two-story frame building heated by stoves. Even with faults such as poor ventilation, in an 1896 report, the facility was complimented on its separation of the sexes, and many of the rooms being furnished with toilets. The building was settling badly, and it was recommended that it get a new foundation.

It had eight people living there in 1910, four men and four women. In 1920 there were 27 men and six women. In 1930 there were 58 men and 10 women. In a 1936 Michigan inspection report, with 49 men and seven women living on the farm, the facility was said to be "well-done."

The Ogemaw County Poor Farm in the 1920's

CHAPTER SIXTY-SIX

Ontonagon County Poor Farm

Ontonagon County is in the northern Upper Peninsula and was set aside in 1843 and organized in 1846. The Ontonagon River runs through the county, and the county and its county seat were both named for it. It is on Lake Superior and east of the Minnesota border. Area-wise, it is the third largest county of Michigan, and the third least populous.

In 1855 the Poor Farm was established for indigent miners and lumberjacks. The Ontonagon Poor Farm was located three miles east of Ontonagon, the county seat, on M-38. It was a two-story frame building and had a detached hospital wing. It had no bathing facilities, heating was by stoves, there was poor ventilation, and the sexes were housed separately.

The residents who were able worked on the farm, with oats, hay, and potatoes as the main crops. In the 1870s Poles made up a large portion of the population—until the 1890s when the Finns became the majority ethnic group.

In 1910 the Ontonagon County Poor Farm in Ontonagon had 15 residents, 14 men and one woman. In 1920 there 16 men and no women, and in 1925 there was again 16 men and no women. In 1930 there were 44 men, and in 1938 there were 36 men and one woman.

The Ontonagon County Poor Farm had an award-winning exhibit in the Upper Peninsula State Fair in 1928. Richard Langford was an explorer and famed pioneer who discovered iron reserves. He died while living at the Poor Farm and was buried in the Potter's Field. In 1958 the Ontonagon County Historical Society placed a marker on his grave.

In 1945 the farm was closed, and the residents were moved to other state facilities.

Ontonagon County Poor Farm

*The Ontonagon Poor Farm main building closed
in 1945 and has not been used since.*

CHAPTER SIXTY-SEVEN

Osceola County Home

Osceola County was established in 1840 as "Unwattin County" and is in the "middle of the Mitten," the Lower Peninsula of Michigan. The name was changed in 1843 to Osceola, after a Seminole First Nation Chief.

The County Home (Poor House) for Osceola County was located two and a half miles from the Village of Sears. Sears was a medium-sized Amish farming community located in the northwest portion of Orient Township, between the highway of U.S. 10 and what was then the Pere Marquette Railway line.

The County Home's main building was a two-story frame building that was heated by stoves. There were no bathing facilities, and ventilation was poor. As in most county homes, the sexes were separated.

In 1910, in the Osceola County Home, there were 29 residents, with 18 men and 11 women. In 1920 there were 13 men and 13 women, while in 1930 there were 45 men and 13 women. In 1938 the County Home had 21 men and seven women.

Osceola County Home

Osceola County Farm Cemetery

CHAPTER SIXTY-EIGHT

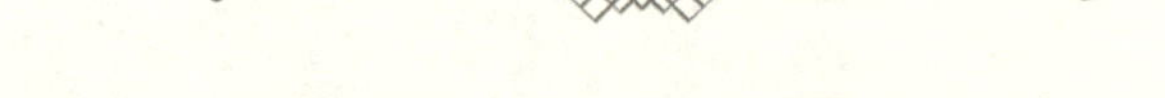

Oscoda County Poorhouse

Oscoda was first set aside in 1840, but no governing bodies appeared until 1881. It is the least populous county in the Lower Peninsula and is part of the Au Sable Forest. The county seat is Mio, an unincorporated community.

In Oscoda County there was no poor house for many years, even though the Oscoda County Board of Supervisors purchased 320 acres of land to be used for a county farm in 1869. From 1920 through 1929 there was only one man listed in the state reports. From 1930 to 1938 the reports state that Oscoda County did not have a poorhouse, probably due to a lack of paupers.

CHAPTER SIXTY-NINE

Otsego County Poorhouse

Otsego County was set aside in 1840 and organized in 1875. It is in the upper part of the Lower Peninsula.

The Poorhouse of Otsego County was established in 1882 and was located about two miles from the county seat, Gaylord, at Meecher and Allis Roads, in Livingston Township. There was a two-story frame house with a wing and the sexes had separate dormitories. Bathing facilities, sewerage, and ventilation were judged lacking in an 1896 report, but it was noted that the building had improved its foundation, chimneys, and cellar since a previous inspection. It was stated that the "house is in excellent condition and much cleaner."

In 1896 a lady that lived in the Otsego County Poorhouse moved to the Genesee Poor House. When she was kicked out of the Genesee home for not being a resident, she was returned to Otsego County. However, she was left without a home when Otsego County rejected her also. It was usually decided that an indigent first went to the county of their parents, or their birth county. Marriage to someone from a different county also complicated which poorhouse a person would be assigned to.

In Gaylord, Otsego County, the 1910 poorhouse population was nine people—seven men and two women. In 1920 there were nine men and two women. In 1930, there were 17 men and one woman, and in 1938 there were 20 men and four women living in the Poorhouse.

The facility closed in 1952 after a 70-year history.

Otsego County Poorhouse

CHAPTER SEVENTY

Ottawa County Infirmary

The last Poor Farm of Michigan was probably the one in Ottawa County—which didn't close until the 1980s! Located five miles from Coopersville, the farm/infirmary evolved into the "Community Haven."

The original Poor Farm building originated2aq in the late 1850s as a business establishment named the Midway Inn. It had a farm, and when it went out of business in the 1880s, it was purchased by the county to be used as a poor farm for the community. The Midway Inn building later became a laundry and lasted until 1956, when it was demolished.

The Ottawa County Poor Farm started in 1884 with a new wing added in 1923. An 1896 report noted that it was a three-story brick building with bathrooms and hot-water heating, although the water supply was said to be inadequate. The house needed fire extinguishers and fire escapes. Sewerage and ventilation were reportedly good, and the house was said to be clean and well-cared for.

In 1910 the Poor Farm in Coopersville (later Eastmanville) had 31 residents—24 men and 7 women and 265 acres. If an inmate needed extra care they were sent to a separate institution, the Ottawa County Asylum. In 1920 the facility was hit by a tornado; on the bright side it received electricity in 1927. A smoking ban was also put in place in 1927. During the Great Depression years of the 1930s, there were 84 residents at the farm.

In 1957 the facility had *two* TV sets.

As the 1960s dawned, most of the Poorhouse and Poor Farm facilities in Michigan had closed. However, the Ottawa County

Department of Social Services continued to operate what had been the Poor Farm, renaming it the Ottawa Infirmary, and then *Community Haven* in the early 1970s. The innovative program was mostly run by the residents, who were developmentally disabled, elderly, or mentally ill. The Keepers in 1970 and beyond were Glen and Sara Collision, who treated all the residents like one big family.

Everybody at the facility had a job, whether it was gathering eggs, working in the fields, or helping in the kitchen. Some helped train the Leader Dogs for the Blind that the facility was responsible for. The facility had a breeding house where parakeets for pet shops were raised.

The residents lived two to a room in the otherwise spacious facility. Residents were treated to frequent trips outside the facility, including movies and recreation such as bowling or dancing. There were even hayrides in the autumn.

Not every resident of the home was indigent. One person who spent his twilight years living at the Poor Farm was Judge David Fletcher Hunter, who voluntarily lived in the home and paid his own expenses. He was also a well-known poet.

In 1980 the Community Haven residents sued to challenge a 1939 law originally passed to discourage county farms. The law stated that no state funds could flow to county institutions. The residents won a small settlement.

Some groups objected to the Community Haven concept, saying that the residents need to get out in the world more. Near the end of its day the facility was considered more of a nursing home than a poorhouse and was shuttered in 2000. Many others defended the concept, until lack of funding forced it to close. The remaining residents were sent to group homes.

After 130 years of continuous service, the longest in the United States, the building was demolished shortly after closing, although there were still a few outbuildings left standing.

In 2000 the area was repurposed as the Eastmanville County Farm Park at 7851 Leonard Road. In 2004, the historical society did an investigation of the Poor Farm Cemetery and identified 64 people buried there. Their names were all inscribed on a plaque displayed at the cemetery.

Ottawa County Poor Farm

CHAPTER SEVENTY-ONE

Presque Isle County Poorhouse

Presque Isle County was set aside in 1840 and a county government established in 1871. It is located on a peninsula jutting out from the eastern, middle part of the Lower Peninsula.

Since the County of Presque Isle didn't have a government until 1871 (and then was reorganized in 1876), it didn't open its poorhouse until after the rest of Michigan's counties.

In 1910 the County Poorhouse, located in Rogers City, had 15 residents, 12 men and three women. In 1920 there were eight men and one woman, and in 1925 there were 19 men and five women. In 1930 there were 22 men and eight women; in 1935 there were 21 men and six women, and in 1938 there were 22 men and seven women.

A 1936 State of Michigan report unfortunately pronounced it "filthy."

CHAPTER SEVENTY-TWO

Roscommon County Poor Farm

Roscommon County was set aside in 1840 as "Mikenauk County" and changed its name to Roscommon, after a county in Ireland, in 1843. It is in the middle of the Lower Peninsula. Houghton Lake and Higgins Lake are within the county.

The County Poor Farm in the City of Roscommon had two residents in 1910, both men. In 1920 there were five men and one woman. In 1925 there were 20 men and no women, while in 1930 there were nine men and one woman.

In 1930 the state recommended that the institution be closed "for economy." However, there were reports of Poor Farm residents throughout the 1930s, usually averaging five men and one or two women.

CHAPTER SEVENTY-THREE

Saginaw County Almshouse

Saginaw County Almshouse/Poor Farm

The Almshouse was erected in 1891 for $19,922, the lowest of seven bids received. The Saginaw County Almshouse was a farm located six miles from the City of Saginaw.

According to an 1896 report, the building was a two-story brick building with a high basement, steam heating, good ventilation, excellent bathing facilities, an ample water supply with its own water tower, and good drainage. Men and women were separately housed.

There was an "insane house," a one-story detached building, which was refurbished in the 1890s, to house the mentally ill.

Although the 1896 report complained that the facility was too many stories tall for indigents, requiring lots of walking upstairs, the report pronounced that there was "no better county house in the state, and it is well-kept."

In 1910 there were 79 residents, 57 men and 22 women. In 1922 the Poor Farm Keeper was accused of withholding food to the residents that had been grown on the farm. According to a Detroit

Free Press article, "chicken and ham and butter and eggs" disappeared from the farm and "never appeared on the table."

Things were eventually smoothed out and in 1936 the Almshouse was once again cited for good performance by the state.

CHAPTER SEVENTY-FOUR

St. Clair County Poor Farm

In 1869 the St. Clair County Poorhouse and Farm was first established in Smith's Creek, which was the county seat at the time. In 1873 it was moved to Goodells and by 1881 there were 72 residents, 58 men and 14 women. Thirteen were under 16 years of age. The residents included four lunatics and two mutes. The county also supported four people in the Deaf and Dumb Institute and one in the Blind Institute.

An 1896 Michigan inspection report said that the poorhouse was at Goodells Station, and that it was a two-story brick building with a high basement, making the building seem like three stories. Separation of the sexes was practiced in the house but not outside in the yard. The facility had good bathing facilities, a good water supply, but bad ventilation and drainage.

The report stated that much-needed fire escapes had been installed and new bath tubs, new floors, and necessary repairs had been made.

It was said that many of the Poor Farm residents worked seasonal jobs in the warmer months and came to stay at the Poor Farm in the winter. One winter there were 129 people living at the Poor Farm. The farm averaged about 65 residents year-round (and more in the winter).

In 1910 the Poor Farm had 63 people, 46 men and 17 women. It was located on County Park Drive—across from the County Park (it was also called Pauper Avenue). Nearby was the Goodells Poor Farm Cemetery.

In 1914 the building caught on fire and all 73 residents were saved "in a heroic way," as stated by the *Port Huron Times Herald*. The residents were put up in makeshift quarters in the Maccabees Hall in Goodells until a new house was completed in June 1915.

After it was the Poor Farm, the building became a nursing home in 1961, and in 1962 it was renamed the St. Clair County Medical Centre. The facility was valued at $15,567 in 1981.

In 1992 it closed and then in 1993 the building was torn down. The land became the County fairgrounds and the barns part of the County Farm Museum.

The St. Clair County Poor Farm in Goodells, Michigan

CHAPTER SEVENTY-FIVE

St. Joseph County Poorhouse

In July 1848, St. Joseph County bought a County Poor Farm in Sturgis for $2,800. It had 139 acres of land; 79 acres improved. In an 1896 inspection it was stated that the poorhouse was located about a mile and a half from Sturgis.

Located in what then a new, two-story brick building, it had steam heat, two bath rooms, separation of the sexes, and a good water supply and drainage. The only fault mentioned was that the ventilation appeared a little defective. The Poor Commissioner commented, "This in most regards is a model poorhouse."

In 1910 there were 35 residents, 27 men and 9 women.

In 1914 a St. Joseph resident contracted leprosy and a controversy developed about putting him in the Poor Farm. County residents felt that by putting him into the facility he might give the disease to others. Also, the facility felt that his presence would "demoralize" the other residents. The leper ended up being sent to a leper colony out-of-state.

The St. Joseph Poorhouse cemetery is named the "County Infirmary Cemetery."

The St. Joseph County Home

St. Joseph County Poor House and Infirmary

CHAPTER SEVENTY-SIX

The Sanilac County Poor Farm

Sanilac County's Poor Farm was located three miles north of Lexington, at that time the county seat. It consisted of 120 acres and the main building was built in 1868 for about $3,300. Prior to opening the Poor Farm, members of the community had been paid by the county to house paupers.

The facility had several farm buildings on the property. The farm produced the resident's food, bringing down the cost to house each pauper to about $1.50 per week. The farm possessed horses to cultivate the land and had hogs and dairy cows. The hogs were quartered in the basement.

The farm raised just about all the food the residents needed. Extra milk was sold to the creamery. The farm had apple orchards and raised chickens for the eggs and meat. Campbell's Soup would purchase the old roosters and laying hens at the end of the year. What the farm didn't use, they sold. Extra eggs were sold to the Mills Grocery and extra milk went to the Gold Seal Dairy in Croswell. Skim milk was given to the calves.

The Poor Farm was governed by a County Supervisor of the Poor. When the Poor Farm was established in 1868, the average number of paupers was 14 at a time. In the 1870 U.S. Census there were 11 farm residents—3 were from the area and 8 were "foreign," which usually meant they came from Canada. Besides the Poor Farm residents, 47 other county people received aid during the year. The total expense for 1870 was $3,145.

By 1883, records show that 284 Sanilac County residents received some outside assistance, costing the county $3,407 for the year, in addition to the $1,475 it cost to operate the poor farm.

Men and women were housed separately. There was a wooden building for the men's quarters, and they slept on the second floor, mostly three to a room—although there were a few "single" rooms. There was a brick building that housed the women and they slept on the third floor. All the women had their own separate room.

In both the men's and the women's dormitories there was a single jail cell—used by the Sheriff as overflow for when the County Jail was full. The cells could also be used to house residents who "acted up."

Heat was through a register providing steam heat from the coal-powered boiler. In the winter when the heat was needed, one of the residents named Ira moved into the boiler building and maintained the heat. He had a bed by the generator and would stay there until spring when the heat was turned off.

One time a female resident was put into one of the jail cells when she was unruly. She continued to act up and tore the steam register out—scalding herself to death!

The farm received electricity long before most other farms in the area. A generator and battery set-up were used until the Rural Electrification Project provided power lines to the property. Electricity allowed for many things, but primarily for refrigeration so the farm could slaughter and store their own meat.

There was a separate building for the Keeper and his family. The hired hands, guests, and the Keeper and his family all used the same dining room. The residents had their own separate dining area.

An 1896 report said that it was a two-story brick building with a basement. Sewerage was good and there was a good supply of water, but a lack of bathing facilities. The report stated that "the building is old and poorly planned but in good condition." It was further stated that the house was very clean, and the paupers well cared for.

The farm was subject to regular and routine state inspections and usually received positive appraisals. One of the few problems mentioned (in 1900) was the lack of a place to bathe. Residents were required to bathe at least once a week.

The Sanilac Poor Farm was on County Farm Road and had its own cemetery near the intersection with Wixsom Road. It is rumored there are graves just south of the remaining barn. Some inmates were buried in the nearby Long Township Cemetery.

During the Great Depression in the 1930s, the Poor Farm averaged about 40 residents. In these years the residents farmed and canned 2,000 half-gallon jars of raspberries and 2,000 half-gallon of strawberries every year, as well as 20 bushels of peaches.

During the times there was pie on the menu, the facility baked 20 pies at a time, and when baking cookies, they would make 500. There were many varieties of cookies, including sugar with a raisin in the middle, and molasses with a spoonful of jelly in the center.

Vegetables were stored underground for the winter. The farm received 1,000 baby chickens each spring. They also had ten to twelve milk cows. They had refrigeration space to store four hogs at a time, so that was the number they always slaughtered.

The facility had a washroom for the laundry with several wringer-type washing machines. After washing, the clothes were put on one of three sets of clotheslines. There were two hired women to help with laundry and kitchen duties and one hired man to oversee the farm workers. It was the job of the female inmates to wash the dishes each day.

Plowing the fields was done with horse teams. The farm eventually got a Farmall M Tractor.

Inmates were taken to Foley's Market on Friday nights where some of the residents would secretly purchase alcohol. Card games were one of the main diversions.

Tobacco was raised for a time, but grain was the primary crop since it could provide feed for the horses and cows and would give them straw for bedding. Since the grain raised was used for animal feed, they didn't mill flour or bake their own bread, buying it instead.

The Poor Farm closed and was sold in 1958. Today there are a few buildings still standing, along with a collapsing barn. A stone that says "County Farm" remains in front of the former facility.

Sanilac Co. Poor Farm on County Farm Road

Sanilac County Poor Farm

CHAPTER SEVENTY-SEVEN

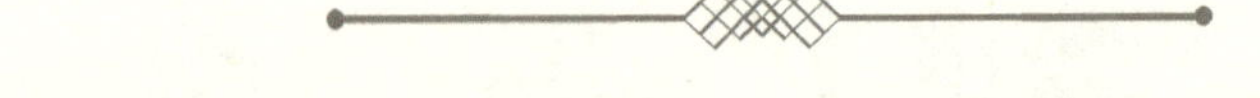

Schoolcraft County Poor House

There is a scarcity of information about the Schoolcraft County Poor House, located in Manistique in the UP, just as there is about most of the poorhouses and farms of Michigan. This is because it was common practice to destroy poorhouse and poor farm records every few years or so. The reasons given were usually that it was embarrassing information and destroying it prevented undesirable information to be readily available. This was despite the fact that many of the poorhouse notes made their way to the newspapers.

An 1896 report stated that the present Schoolcraft County Poor House was one and a half miles from the village limits of Manistique, the county seat of Schoolcraft County. It was a one-story frame house, with a detached medical building. It had bathing facilities, separation of men and women, a good supply of water but needed sewerage, and was heated by stoves.

Despite the good farming, the Poor House Committee selected a different place to move to in 1904. It was located, according to the records, at the "northeast corner of the northwest quarter of the southeast quarter of section 11, township 41 north range sixteen west, Michigan, running thence west 197 feet, thence south 221 feet, thence east 197 feet, thence north 221 feet to place of beginning. To be used by said county as a location for a County Poor House." This location was previously the Elk Street Lodge. A building was built on the property and in 1908 opened as the Poor House.

According to an 1886 report, the Schoolcraft County Poorhouse produced larger crops than all the farms in the area, even though the soil was not considered very good. The farm produced "the nicest potatoes, largest turnips, weightiest cabbage, longest radishes, beets and the biggest squashes…The orchard, although quite young, bears some of the handsomest apples grown; smaller fruits of all kinds are grown with success."

In 1910 there were 22 people in the Poor House system in Schoolcraft County, 21 of them were male, with one female. In 1920 the count was 30 men and six women. In 1930 there were 40 men and four women and in 1938 the institution had 50 men and five women.

After the Schoolcraft County Poor House closed, the main building became a bed and breakfast.

CHAPTER SEVENTY-EIGHT

Shiawassee County Poor House

The Shiawassee County Poor House was in Caledonia Township, Michigan, two miles from the county seat of Corunna. It was organized in 1837 by appointing three men as Superintendents of the Poor. For a few years the county made appropriations for the care of the few poor in the area, but in 1847 the need for a Poor House became greater as more poor people moved to the county. A poorhouse was built on 80 acres of land in Caledonia Township. In 1858 the buildings were deemed to be in poor shape and $1,500 was appropriated for updates and repairs. The construction was finished in January 1859.

In 1879 the farm had 32 residents with no death records recorded until 1887. In 1849 the value of the produce of the farm was given as $163.25. In 1910 there were 15 men and 22 women and in 1920 there were 42 men and 16 women. In 1930 there were 43 men and 24 women and in 1938 there were 45 men and 10 women.

In 1896 a state report reported that the Poorhouse was an old two-story frame building, with a separate building for old men and one for "filthy inmates." It was stated that the building was "badly arranged," but noted that it had a good fire escape. Also noted was bath rooms, separation of men and women, a fair supply of water, and good drainage. It was, overall, "in most excellent condition." The farm closed in 1955 and the residents were transferred to other institutions.

Shiawassee Poor Farm Cemetery, aka the County Farm Cemetery

CHAPTER SEVENTY-NINE

Tuscola County Infirmary

The 1896 Michigan Welfare Report stated that the Tuscola County Poor House was a mile from the county seat of Caro and consisted of two brick two-story buildings. One housed male inmates and the other housed female inmates and the Keeper's family. The men and women were allowed to mingle in the yard.

There were bathing facilities and a good water supply and sewerage. Ventilation was somewhat lacking, and it needed fire escapes. Still, the commissioner who did the inspection said that it was "one of the best-kept in the state."

The Tuscola County Infirmary in Caro had 40 residents in 1910, 15 men and 22 women. In 1920 the number of men was 33 and there were 18 women; in 1925 there were 29 men and 17 women, in 1930 56 men and 18 women, and in 1938 there were 38 men and five women.

In 1930 a deaf-mute man who had walked away from his home 25 years before was discovered in the Tuscola County Infirmary. A nephew that had always wanted to solve the mystery of what happened to him discovered him and reunited him with the family.

In 1948 a "hired man" at the Infirmary who worked on the farm was fired due to committing assault and battery on the 16-year-old son of the Keeper of the Infirmary while he was working on the farm—knocking him down and kicking him. The Keeper himself was fired (allowed to resign) not long after for abusing residents after losing his temper.

Tuscola County Poorhouse/Infirmary

CHAPTER EIGHTY

Van Buren County Poor House/County Home

The Van Buren County Home in Hartford was built in 1886. It was a brick building that replaced a previous wooden poorhouse that burned down. The blaze had killed 17 inmates of the house.

In 1896 the Poor House was housed three miles from Lawrence in a two-story, stone building with a high basement, making the structure to appear to have almost three stories. It had good bathing facilities, with a good water supply and drainage, and it was heated by furnaces and well-ventilated. The report concluded that the county home was "good in every respect."

The farm was self-sustaining, with every able-bodied resident helping to work the fields. In 1910 there were 47 residents, 32 men and 15 women. Men and women were separately housed. In 1920 there were 38 men and eight women and in 1930 there were 48 men and 30 women.

The Van Buren County Home closed in 1952 and was converted to office space. The land around the Home became the County Fairgrounds. In 1958 the welfare offices were moved to other quarters and the building stood vacant for 14 years.

In 1972 the Van Buren County Board of Commissioners voted to give the building to the Van Buren County Historical Society, who converted it to a museum. In 1977 the site became a registered Michigan Historic Site.

Van Buren County Home, later Museum

CHAPTER EIGHTY-ONE

Washtenaw County Poor Farm and Infirmary

The paupers of Washtenaw County went to the Washtenaw County Poor Farm in Pittsfield Township, three miles from Ann Arbor. It was located near Platt Road, which was called "Pauper's Alley."

The property, 128 acres, 90 cultivated, of "gravelly soil" was purchased in 1837 at a cost of $1,200. The buildings were erected shortly after, the main one costing $4,350. In 1848 the produce produced by the farm was worth about $500.

Heat was by steam, and bathing, required at least once a week, was done in tubs. Residents were required to work a bit every day and were otherwise well-fed and clothed, according to state reports of 1893. The Poor Farm Cemetery was not far from the grounds.

An 1896 state inspection said that the main building was a three-story building, with good bathing facilities, water supply, and drainage. Heat was by steam and the building was well-ventilated with good fire escapes. The house had been repainted and repaired. Medical facilities were provided. The report said that the house was "in good clean condition."

Washtenaw County Poor Farm and Washtenaw Infirmary, 1970

The farm was worked by the inmates and featured livestock and an orchard of apple, cherry and peach trees. Vegetables and grains were grown. The farm helped pay the expenses when they sold the grain, as well as provide for most of the Poor Farm's food.

Although the insane were sent to the Eastern Michigan State Asylum in Pontiac, the "idiotic" were housed at the farm. Males and females had separate sick sections when they were ill and were attended by people of the same sex. The Poor Farm had its own teacher for school-age children. In 1910 there were 52 people housed in the Ann Arbor facility, 37 men and 15 women.

In 1917 a hospital, or infirmary, was built to house permanently disabled residents and for sick inmates. By the social welfare systems of the 1930s, the Poor Farm population became mainly a home for people that couldn't live on their own. Washtenaw County ended its milk operation in 1951, auctioning off the cattle and the dairy and milking equipment. The infirmary stayed open until 1971 and was torn down in 1979. The site of the Poor Farm is now known as Poor Farm Park.

CHAPTER EIGHTY-TWO

Eloise — The Wayne County Poorhouse/Almshouse and the Wayne County General Hospital and Infirmary

The original main building at Eloise Asylum

Probably the most famous poorhouse, at least in Michigan, was the one in Wayne County, most commonly known as Eloise. The subject of books and movies, it is best known as an insane asylum although it also included a poorhouse, a tuberculosis sanitarium, an infirmary, a general hospital, and a farm.

The Eloise story began in 1828 when Detroit and Wayne County appointed Directors of the Poor and wrote a proposal for a building that was to be built that would "provide suitable reception, use and accommodation of the poor of the county, and also for the reception of vagrants, vagabonds, lewd, idle, or disorderly persons, stubborn servants, common drunkards, common nightwalkers (prostitutes), pilferers, persons wanton and lascivious in speech, conduct and behavior, common railers or brawlers, such as neglect their calling and employment, misspend what they earn, and do not provide for themselves and their families, and who shall be convicted or sentenced to hard labor for any offense, under any law of the Territory, to said House of Reformation, to serve the poor therein; to provide all things necessary for the lodging, maintenance of said poor, to provide also separate quarters and all things necessary for the reception, lodging, and maintenance and employment of such offenders as may be sentenced to labor, to serve the poor in the said House of Restitution (the Poorhouse facility)."

Besides creating one of the longest run-on sentences of the 19th Century, the statute would seem to make anyone eligible to be sent to the Poorhouse, by force if necessary, especially when allowed for individuals to decide what standards by which a person was duly providing support for his family.

The most grievous provision of the proposal was the part that stated that people convicted of crimes would be sentenced to provide hard labor in service of the poor, or similar punishment. In other words, convicts would be housed with the poor. The proposal did not pass but neither did the need for a Poorhouse. In 1830 action was taken to house the poor and keep the criminals in a separate prison.

The Black Horse Tavern, which became the Poorkeeper's quarters

The 1930 Wayne County Poorhouse (also referred to as the Wayne County Almshouse) was first established near the intersection and northwest corner of (Fort) Gratiot and Mt. Elliott Roads in Hamtramck Township. This was about two miles from what were then the Detroit City limits.

By 1838 the Hamtramck building became overcrowded and run-down. Inexpensive land was purchased in Nankin Township, located on the Old Chicago Road which led from Detroit to Chicago, now known as Michigan Avenue. The Black Horse Tavern was on the property and had been a stagecoach stop. The tavern was closed and the building itself became the Poorkeeper's quarters.

Eloise was on the north side of Michigan Avenue, between Henry Ruff and Merriman Roads, in the present-day City of Westland, a town named for a shopping center within its city limits which opened in 1965.

The Wayne County Poorhouse complex became large enough to warrant its own post office in 1894. The post office and complex were named "Eloise" after the four-year-old daughter of Freeman B. Dickinson, the President of the Board of the Supervisors of the Poor for Wayne County. The closest train, the Michigan Central Railroad, had a stop named "Eloise" and the name started to be the common name used for the entire complex. Eloise Dickinson lived until 1982 and is buried in Detroit's Woodlawn Cemetery.

Four-year-old Eloise Peterson (married name Davock),
namesake of Eloise, with her St. Bernard

The Eloise property consisted of 280 acres, 100 of which were improved. When it came time to move to the new facility from Hamtramck Township, only 35 paupers went. There were 111 others who refused to go into the "awful wilderness" and stayed around Detroit.

The main building of Eloise was built in 1845 at the cost of $4,609.00. Eloise grew into what was by far the largest poorhouse facility in Michigan. It evolved into a community with its own post office (and later, its own zip code, 48141), laundries, an amusement hall, a cannery, both trolley and railroad stations, fire and police stations, and a school. There were 16 kitchens serving about 30,000 meals every day.

In a portion of the northeast corner of the basement were two cells which were used for unruly inmates and drunks. Sometimes the insane would be housed there. As the insane population grew, other alternatives, including straitjackets, were used.

Insane patients being restrained with straitjackets

Rev. Martin Kundig

Reverend Martin Kundig became the first Superintendent of the Poor after the first County House was built. He proved an inspiration to the entire county when he tirelessly and fearlessly attended victims of the Cholera Epidemics of 1832 and 1834.

After the cholera epidemics, many orphans whose parents died of cholera in the epidemic came to live in the Poorhouse. Eloise established a school for them and had its own separate school district by 1839. It was originally School District #10 of Nankin. In 1871 it was designated the State Public School.

Although Eloise would grow to be a renowned psychiatric facility, it wasn't until 1841 that the County House began distinguishing between rational and insane patients. In the early 1840s a "crazy house" was built to house violent and insane inmates. The crazy house went from being a simple log cabin, to a frame, two-story facility built in 1859.

Reportedly the first floor was for "colored inmates," while on the second floor there were cells with chains fastened to the wall for securing the violently insane. In 1858 a separate building was erected for black inmates. Eloise was segregated throughout most of its history.

The Michigan Asylum for the Insane was established at Kalamazoo in 1859, but because it was often filled to capacity and would only take the "curably insane," Eloise established the separate Wayne County Asylum in 1868 and it included the incurably insane. In 1885 the west wing was added for violent and insane females.

The farms of Eloise were fruitful. The farm buildings included a piggery, a tobacco curing building, barns, root cellars, and greenhouses. There were men's and women's dormitories and the facility had its own powerhouse. There were at one time 78 buildings.

The cow, horse, and hay barns of Eloise Poor Farm

The value of the Eloise farm crops in 1886 was estimated at $600 per year and $60 for vegetables. Wool, butter, and cheeses brought in $108. Most of what was grown was fed to the inmates and farm animals. When there was an excess it was sold. Eloise sold so much milk it had its own milk bottles which had "Eloise" labels.

In 1858 the "pest house" was built, where people with contagious diseases would be sent. This included smallpox, which broke out among the inmates in 1872.

The facility grew and by the late 1860s it had grown to 902 acres and housed over 10,000 residents. The staff numbered over 2,000. One building, Kelley Hall, could house 7,000 residents. Eloise reached its peak population during the Great Depression; after the 1930s the population went down.

In 1887 the entire Eloise facility changed to steam heat, as three gigantic boilers provided the steam. An electric light plant provided electricity starting in 1894.

In 1895 a separate laundry building was erected. An 1896 state inspection report described the main building as a three-story brick building that cost $56,000. The buildings had separation of the sexes, good bathing facilities, water supply, ventilation and sewerage, good fire protection and escapes, and hospital rooms for the sick. There were no private rooms, only large dormitory-type rooms. The state inspection report concluded that the facility was well-maintained and that the residents were well-cared for.

In 1903 tents were erected on the property for tuberculosis patients, intentionally taking them outdoors as part of their treatment. A separate dormitory and separate kitchen was also built for them.

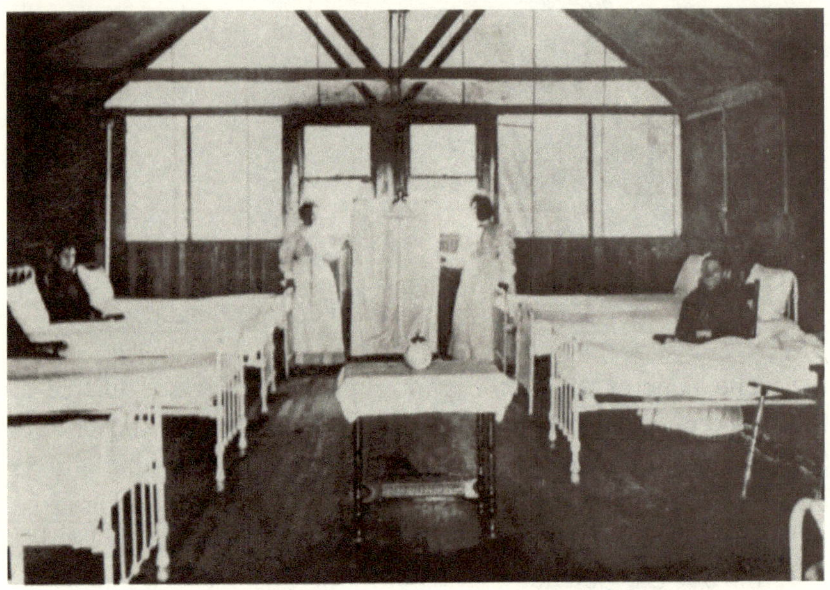

The Eloise Tuberculosis Tent c1904

During the early 1900s Eloise was the largest psychiatric facility in the United States. It evolved greatly from keeping the insane chained up in the second story of the piggery, to becoming one of the most progressive medical facilities in the nation. The mental health facilities were officially named Eloise Hospital in 1911 by the Board of Superintendents of the Poor. Previously the complex of buildings was known as the Wayne County Asylum.

Michigan passed *Public Act #21 of 1911*, which changed the names of all buildings in the state that were officially called "asylums." It was decided that all asylums would henceforth be "hospitals." Thus, in 1911, the mental asylum of Eloise became the mental hospital of Eloise.

Most of the buildings of Eloise were frame (wood) and so they had their own fire department, along with a sewer department, water department, carpenter shop, and others added in the 1890s. An artificial lake was built in 1890.

The Eloise Fire Department in 1912

The Tubercular Sanitarium, built in 1911

In 1912 a larger main facility was built. The entire second floor was an entertainment hall, complete with bowling alley. This was not for the use of the inmates but constructed to "keep good employees."

Eloise Hospital pioneered the use of Music Therapy as a treatment for mental problems, and the use of X-Rays. Eloise also had the first kidney dialysis in Michigan, pioneered the use of radium for cancer treatment, and "open air" treatment for tuberculosis.

Farm operations continued until 1958, and after that the facility purchased its food outside the facility. Some of the psychiatric buildings started closing around 1973 and in 1977 the hospital complex also started closing. By 1986 all of the medical buildings were closed and vacant.

After a lot of vandalism, most of the Eloise buildings were torn down, although five remained in 2019: the bakery, the powerhouse, and the "D" block of dormitories, the commissary, and the firehouse. D Building (the Kay Beard Building) houses a small Eloise museum with artifacts from the asylum. There is also the Eloise Cemetery.

Until 1892 the unclaimed poor were buried in a cemetery that was often plundered by Ann Arbor medical students for the use of cadavers—until a law was passed legally *giving* the unclaimed poor bodies to the medical school for educational purposes.

The Kay Beard Building in 2018.

In 1982 a fire destroyed many of the buildings. Afterwards, most of the property was sold to Ford Motor Company in the late 1980s. Today there is a strip mall, condominiums, and a golf course on the site where Eloise stood, besides the dwindling remaining buildings.

In 2015 the main Eloise building, long rumored to be haunted, and the remaining 28 acres was put up for sale for $1.5 million dollars. In 2017 the movie "Eloise" was partially shot there. In 2018 the property was sold to developers who will create senior housing in the main, Kay Beard Building. The sale also includes the bakery, the decommissioned power plant, and the fire station.

The Wayne County Poor House was known as Eloise, named after the daughter of Eloise's first postmaster.

The Eloise Firehouse in 2015

The Eloise Bakery in 2015

CHAPTER EIGHTY-THREE

Wexford County Poor Farm/Almshouse

In 1871, the first Poor Farm in the county was in Colfax Township, fourteen miles from Cadillac, the county seat and closest railroad station. A large two-story building was erected on the property. Later, twelve dormitories were built.

When the Superintendent of the Poor moved in to take care of the Root family when the breadwinner was put in jail, it was referred to as the Root Farm and circa 1880, the county ended up owning the farm and using it as the Poor Farm, replacing the previous farm. The vacated farm was sold, foreclosed on, and sold again. The Root Farm buildings were renovated.

An 1896 report said that the facility was a two-story frame building with two wings, one for males and the other for females. Inmates could mingle in the yard. There were good bathing facilities, with a good water supply, ventilation, drainage, and sewerage. Heat was by furnace and the building had fire escapes. It was judged, "all in most excellent condition."

The Wexford place for the poor was alternately called the Poor Farm or the County Almshouse. It included separate quarters for the Keeper of the Poor and his family. The farm moved to Haring Township in later years.

In 1910 there were 26 people, 22 men and 4 women. In 1920 there were 33 men and seven women. In 1930 there were 52 men and 11 women.

CONCLUSION

Right or wrong, the Poorhouse system had its advantages and disadvantages. Originally meant as a means to care for the less fortunate, in the hands of caring and well-meaning caretakers the system worked well. But the system could be very hellish for residents of poorhouses and farms with cruel Poormasters.

From general cruelty to forced sterilization, many examples abound of the darker side of the Poor House system. It is judged to be a blessing that poorhouses do not exist to the extent that they did in the 18th through the 20th Centuries, even though similar institutions do exist today. One can't help but wonder if the many poor and homeless people on the streets wouldn't prefer a warm bed and meal at a Poorhouse!

Most of the original poorhouse structures of Michigan are gone although a very few remain. The old Poor Farm in Manistique is now a bed and breakfast. The Lake County Poorhouse still stands on a lonely country road as does the Isabella County Poorhouse. The Sanilac County Farm still has a few buildings, including a sagging barn and a stone in front identifying it as the County Farm. Some have only the foundations, like the Jackson County poorhouse. Lenawee County has preserved one of its remaining Poor Farm barns and the Van Buren County Home and Hillsdale Poorhouse are both museums!

BIBLIOGRAPHY

Annual Abstract of the Reports of the Superintendents of the Poor in the State of Michigan (1919-1938). Fort Wayne, IN: Fort Wayne Printing Co.

Blakemore, Erin (2018). *Poorhouses Were Designed to Punish People for Their Poverty*. New York: A & E Television Network. Accessed August 3, 2019, from **https://www.history.com/news/in-the-19th-century-*the*-last-place-you-wanted-to-go-was-the-poorhouse**

Boersma, Loekie (2003). *Ottawa County Poor Farm*. Self-published in Marne, Michigan.

Bruce, Isabel Campbell and Edith Eickhoff (1936). *The Michigan Poor Law*. New York, NY: Arno Press.

Carlton, Will (1882). *Over the Hill to the PoorHouse*. New York, NY: Harper and Brothers.

Collin, Rev. Henry P. (1906). A 20th Century History and Biographical Record OF Branch County, Michigan. New York, NY: The Lewis Publishing Company.

Driscoll, Betty S. (2005). *History of the Gratiot County Poor Farm.* New Era, MI: Self-Published.

Fallon, Jerome A. (1989). *The Will Carleton Poorhouse.* Hillsdale, MI: Hillsdale Historical Society.

Fromwiller, Laura & Jan Gillis (2014). *Oakdale: The Lapeer County State Home.* Charleston, N.C.: Arcadia Publishing.

Ibbotson, Patricia (2002). *Eloise: Poorhouse, Farm, Asylum and Hospital 1839-1984.* Charleston, N.C.: Arcadia Publishing.

Index to Paupers Who Received Relief from the Superintendents of the Poor, Iosco County, Michigan: 1869-1934. Oscoda, MI: Huron Shore Genealogical Society.

Index to Poor Farm Inmates, Iosco County, Michigan (1993). Oscoda, MI: Huron Shore Genealogical Society.

Johnson, Heidi (2001). *Angels in the Architecture.* Detroit: Wayne State University Press

Joint Documents of the State of Michigan, Vol. 1 (1896). Lansing, MI: Robert Smith & Co.

Kail, Ronald (1966). *The Collection, Comparison, and Evaluation of Data Concerning 400 Students from Non-Poor Families to Determine Their Specific Need from Education in Sault Ste. Marie, Michigan.* Sault Ste. Marie, MI: Self-Published.

Katz, Michael B. (1996). *In the Shadow of the Poorhouse: A Social History of Welfare in America.* New York, NY: Basicbooks.

Keenan, Stanislas M (1913). *The History of Eloise: Wayne County House, Wayne County Asylum.* Detroit, MI: Thomas Smith Press.

Laws of the State of Michigan Relating the Support of Poor People. (1878). Lansing, MI: W.S. George & Co.

Lynch, Timothy, and Paul Leonard (1991). *A Place to Call Home: The Crisis in Housing for the Poor.* Washington, DC: Center on Budget and Policy Priorities.

Pardon, Joshua and Marjorie Viveen (2017). *The Poor Farm: A Documentary.* (DVD). Big Rapids, MI.

Romig, Walter (1973). *Michigan Place Names: The History of the Founding and the Naming of More than Five Thousand Past and Present Michigan Communities.* Detroit: Wayne State University Press, Great Lakes Books.

Wagner, David (2005). *The Poorhouse: America's Forgotten Institution.* Lanham, MD: Rowman & Littlefield.

Over the Hill to the Poorhouse
Will Carleton (1845–1912)

Over the hill to the poor-house I 'm trudgin' my weary way—
I, a woman of seventy, and only a trifle gray—
I, who am smart an' chipper, for all the years I 've told,
As many another woman that's only half as old.

Over the hill to the poor-house—I can't quite make it clear!
Over the hill to the poor-house—it seems so horrid queer!
Many a step I 've taken a-toilin' to and fro,
But this is a sort of journey I never thought to go.

What is the use of heapin' on me a pauper's shame?
Am I lazy or crazy? am I blind or lame?
True, I am not so supple, nor yet so awful stout;
But charity ain't no favor, if one can live without.

I am willin' and anxious an' ready any day
To work for a decent livin', an' pay my honest way;
For I can earn my victuals, an' more too, I 'll be bound,
If anybody only is willin' to have me round.

Once I was young an' han'some—I was, upon my soul—
Once my cheeks was roses, my eyes as black as coal;
And I can't remember, in them days, of hearin' people say,
For any kind of a reason, that I was in their way.

'T ain't no use of boastin', or talkin' over free,
But many a house an' home was open then to me;
Many a han'some offer I had from likely men,
And nobody ever hinted that I was a burden then.

And when to John I was married, sure he was good and smart,
But he and all the neighbors would own I done my part;
For life was all before me, an' I was young an' strong,
And I worked the best that I could in tryin' to get along.

And so we worked together: and life was hard, but gay,
With now and then a baby for to cheer us on our way;
Till we had half a dozen, an' all growed clean an' neat,
An' went to school like others, an' had enough to eat.

So we worked for the child'rn, and raised 'em every one;
Worked for 'em summer and winter, just as we ought to 've done;
Only perhaps we humored 'em, which some good folks condemn,
But every couple's child'rn 's heap the best to them.

Strange how much we think of our blessed little ones! —
I 'd have died for my daughters, I 'd have died for my sons;
And God he made that rule of love; but when we 're old and gray,
I 've noticed it sometimes somehow fails to work the other way.

Strange, another thing: when our boys an' girls was grown,
And when, exceptin' Charley, they 'd left us there alone;
When John he nearer an' nearer come, an' dearer seemed to be,
The Lord of Hosts he come one day an' took him away from me.

Still I was bound to struggle, an' never to cringe or fall—
Still I worked for Charley, for Charley was now my all;
And Charley was pretty good to me, with scarce a word or frown,
Till at last he went a-courtin' and brought a wife from town.

She was somewhat dressy, an' hadn't a pleasant smile—
She was quite conceity, and carried a heap o' style;
But if I ever tried to be friends, I did with her, I know;
But she was hard and proud, an' I couldn't make it go.

She had an edication, an' that was good for her;
But when she twitted me on mine, 't was carryin' things too fur;
An' I told her once, 'fore company (an' it almost made her sick),
That I never swallowed a grammar, or 'et a 'rithmetic.

So 't was only a few days before the thing was done—
They was a family of themselves, and I another one;
And a very little cottage one family will do,
But I never have seen a house that was big enough for two.
An' I could never speak to suit her, never could please her eye,
An' it made me independent, an' then I didn't try;
But I was terribly staggered, an' felt it like a blow,
When Charley turned ag'in me, an' told me I could go.

I went to live with Susan, but Susan's house was small,
And she was always a-hintin' how snug it was for us all;
And what with her husband's sisters, and what with child'rn three,
'T was easy to discover that there wasn't room for me.

An' then I went to Thomas, the oldest son I 've got,
For Thomas's buildings 'd cover the half of an acre lot;
But all the child'rn was on me—I couldn't stand their sauce—
And Thomas said I needn't think I was comin' there to boss.

An' then I wrote to Rebecca, my girl who lives out West,
And to Isaac, not far from her—some twenty miles at best;
And one of 'em said 't was too warm there for any one so old,
And t' other had an opinion the climate was too cold.

So they have shirked and slighted me, an' shifted me about—
So they have well-nigh soured me, an' wore my old heart out;
But still I 've borne up pretty well, an' wasn't much put down,
Till Charley went to the poor-master, an' put me on the town.

Over the hill to the poor-house—my child'rn dear, good by!
Many a night I 've watched you when only God was nigh;
And God 'll judge between us; but I will al'ays pray
That you shall never suffer the half I do to-day.

ABOUT THE AUTHOR

As a college student, Alan Naldrett started one of the nation's first used record stores on the campus of Michigan State University, where he received his BA degree.

Moving to California, Alan was an insurance agent in the San Francisco Bay Area. From his office in Fremont, California, he sold Farmers, State Farm, Metropolitan, and Prudential Insurance, (not at the same time), and the insurance of other companies. But when he realized he knew more about actuarial tables and loss ratios than vintage automobile companies and ghost towns, he realized it was time for a change.

Relocating back to Michigan, he acquired a couple of Master's Degrees in Library and Information and Archival Science from Wayne State University. He was first a medical librarian and then was an academic librarian at Baker College for more than ten years.

Upon retirement he continued writing books, a practice he started while a reference librarian. He has now written over 20 books, including the *Lost Towns of Eastern Michigan*, the *Lost Car Companies of Detroit*, and *Michigan's C. Harold Wills—The Genius Behind the Model T and the Wills Sainte Claire Automobile*.

Another action Alan has taken up is archival organization. He has arranged historical files for Baker College, Chesterfield Township, the Wills Sainte Claire Museum, the First Congregational Church of New Baltimore, the Chesterfield and New Baltimore Historical Societies, and Green School, among others, usually on a volunteer basis.

Although claiming to know little about vice, Alan is the former Vice-Chairman of the Macomb County Historical Commission and presently, Vice-President of the Chesterfield Library Board of Trustees. A member of the Michigan Historical Society, he has written research articles for the *Michigan History* and *Michigan Chronicle* magazines. A life member of the Chesterfield and New Baltimore Historical Societies and the Wills Sainte Claire Museum, he has conducted many programs and presentations for them, and for history-lovers all over Michigan. He was awarded the Award of Merit by the New Baltimore Historical Society, and the Spirit of Wills Award by the Wills Sainte Claire Museum.

He is also a member of the F Street Blues, a blues band. He can be reached for band bookings, or book presentations at alannaldrett@ gmail.com.

BOOKS BY ALAN NALDRETT

Images of America: Chesterfield Township
Lost Towns of Eastern Michigan
Forgotten Tales of Michigan's Lower Peninsula
Lost Car Companies of Detroit
Michigan's C. Harold Wills
How Detroit Became the Motor City
Great Small Towns of Michigan
Michigan's Great Thumb Fires of 1871 and 1881
Capitalists, Clowns, and Crooks: The Mayors of Detroit
Guide to the Governors and Lieutenant Governors of Michigan
Putting the Vice in the Vice-Presidents
Michigan's Forgotten Celebrities
Michigan's Poorhouses and Poor Farms
The Triumphs and Tragedies of the Orphan Car Companies
Independent Car Companies of the U.S.-State by State
Hidden Hamlets and Vanished Villages

Co-written by Alan Naldrett

Images of America: New Baltimore
Images of America: Ira Township
Images of America: Fraser

New Naldrett Press and Alan Naldrett can be reached at alannaldrett@gmail.com